D1220723

Improving Patterns of Language Usage

Improving Patterns of Language Usage

RUTH I. GOLDEN

English Department, Detroit Central High School

WAYNE STATE UNIVERSITY PRESS

Detroit 1960

Library of Congress catalog card number 60–7261.

Published for the National Council of Teachers of English
by Wayne State University Press.

Third printing, January 1967

To the memory of
Dr. Mary McLeod Bethune

July 10, 1875–May 18, 1955

Preface

This book is the outgrowth of a year spent in the independent study of a most interesting and challenging teaching problem concerning the changing of language patterns. It is an attempt at setting forth the problem and offering a few possible ways to meet it—setting it forth in such a way that teachers can easily understand it—in terms which they can transmit to their high school students.

As a teacher at three different Detroit high schools where the school population consists predominantly of Negro students, I I had observed that many students there, particularly those of a low socio-economic level, frequently used certain non-standard language expressions. Because language is constantly changing, these expressions are now antiquated and awkward in structure. Language functions on many levels, but a pattern of speech containing such expressions, it seemed to me, was unacceptable as good speech for high school students and hindered their social and vocational progress. Present methods of language teaching do help many of them to overcome their deep-rooted habits, but the majority of our students who wish to progress socially and economically need to practice more widely accepted speech patterns; but, first, they must want to make them their own. We are not completely succeeding either in arousing this desire nor in substituting a new set of values regarding language. Many students are impatient with their own social progress. They wish to be accepted by middle-class standards but do not realize the importance of language as a key to that acceptance. The level of language which has served very well for their parents is inadequate for them. They must not be disrespectful of their home language, but the new doors they hope to open turn only to the keys of certain patterns. Since our students want to progress and need to be helped, we must find better teaching techniques.

To learn the exact nature of the problem and how to cope with it, I used a questionnaire directly with eleventh and twelfth grade students in six Detroit high schools. The specific purpose of the questionnaire was to discover the frequency of the use of certain expressions in some high-school communities as compared with others. It was also designed to discover some of the background factors related to these expressions and to determine the motivational forces and types of teaching techniques most popular with students. It reveals language differences only to the extent that any questionnaire can validly do so, for, as Harold B. Allen writes me, there is " only a most irregular relationship between the asked-for grammatical response of a person who uses any non-standard forms at all and the same person's spontaneous and uninhibited language." I discussed a rough draft of the questionnaire with many informed people and their suggestions contributed to the study as well as to its final wording. Leaders of the Urban League and the NAACP approved its use.

My study also involved reading, observing, interviewing, and evaluating. The reading has been mainly on language and language teaching and on various phases of the socio-economic background of students. There is comparatively little published material that deals specifically with this particular language problem. The New York Public Library has the most complete card file of the libraries searched, and the *Readers' Guide to Periodical Literature* has been helpful. I visited thirteen colleges and universities, nineteen high schools, attended five national conventions and six conferences. States covered by these visits include New York, Virginia, Florida, Georgia, Illinois, Michigan, and the District of Columbia. The approximately 120 interviews I had have been augmented by a correspondence of considerable magnitude. (Institutions visited, conventions attended, and persons interviewed are listed in the Appendix.)

Part one delineates the problem, the questionnaire, and its findings. Part two is an attempt to set forth possible ways to meet it and to suggest types of lessons needed. Part three gives examples of remedial lessons and exercises.

To the many people who have contributed to this work I make my grateful acknowledgment. I am indebted to all of them for their time and interest. Although it seems unfair to single out any individuals, my special thanks go to my immediate superiors, Henry Eddy, Helen Hanlon, and A. L. McGrath, and to the following doctors and professors who have advised and encouraged me: Harold B. Allen (University of Minnesota), Henry Lee Smith, Jr. (University of Buffalo), Wilmer K. Trauger (New York State University Teachers College), A. L. Davis (American University American Language Center), William Reitz and Donald Lloyd (Wayne State University), Allison Davis (University of Chicago), Stuart Courtis (Professor Emeritus, University of Michigan), Paul Bagwell and Max S. Smith (Michigan State University), and Nathaniel Tillman (Atlanta University).

I am grateful to the Fund for the Advancement of Education and to the Detroit Board of Education for making this study possible. The Urban League and Mr. Charles H. Mahoney, a former delegate to the United Nations, assisted financially in the cost of computing the questionnaire, which was done through the courtesy of Dr. Arvid W. Jacobson, Director of the Computational Laboratory, Wayne State University. Mr. Max Thompson, Superintendent of the Van Dyke School District, expedited the mimeographing of the questionnaire. For their help I am grateful.

This publication would not have been possible without the interest and encouragement of Dr. J. N. Hook, Executive Secretary of the National Council of Teachers of English, and Dr. Harold A. Basilius, Director of the Wayne State University

Press. I am truly indebted to them and to the editor of the press, Professor Alexander Brede, for his careful attention to detail. My gratitude also extends to Paul Onica for his critical reading, to Genevieve Repeta and Janet Ervin for their typing, and most of all to my husband, David L. Golden, and our daughter, Patricia Gayle Golden, for their patient understanding.

Dr. Mary McLeod Bethune—"the Amazon of God," as Edwin Embree called her—has been a source of energy to me. The love and inspiration she radiated greatly impressed me when I visited her shortly before her death. She was founder of Bethune-Cookman College, Daytona Beach, Florida, and Director of the Negro division of the National Youth Administration under President Franklin Delano Roosevelt. Her life parallels the development of Negro education in America, to which cause she devoted almost super-human effort.

I make no claim to being an authority on language. My statements are based on the language sense I gained by, or perhaps retained after, twenty-five years of secondary school teaching.

R. I. G.

Contents

Tables

PART ONE

A Teaching Problem

1 *Introduction*

In our pursuit of happiness, most of us have found that it does not lie in extremes. Too much of anything may result in as much unhappiness as too little. Happiness lies in a feeling of peace, comfort, and security in the way we adjust to the life around us. A major aim of education is to help individuals to acquire the tools and skills and values necessary for our life adjustments.

Language is one of the most important of these tools since through language we communicate and through communication all else is achieved. As a tool, language has much to do with the measure of security we attain. Although it must be acknowledged that many people achieve a fair measure of economic security without acceptable language, they are exceptional people, perhaps with some unusual talent. In the presence of the cultured, it is questionable how secure they actually feel.

That differences in language do exist must be acknowledged. In classifying them, Charles Carpenter Fries, outstanding authority on language, tells us that there are four large types of differences even if one ignores the little details which distinguish every single person's speech from that of any other.

> First, there are historical differences. . . . Constant change is the outstanding characteristic of a live language used by an intellectually active people. The historical changes do not come suddenly, nor do they affect all the users of a language equally. Thus at any time there will be found those who cling to the older methods and those who use the newer fashion. Many of the dif-

ferences in the language of today find their explanation in this process of historical change. . . .

Second, there are regional differences. . . . Some of the differences we note in the language practices of those about us find their explanation in the fact that the fashions in one community or section of the country do not necessarily develop in others. . . . Such regional differences become especially noticeable when a person from one section of the country moves into another bringing with him the peculiar fashions of the district from which he comes. In the new community these language differences challenge attention and give rise to questions of correctness and preference.

Third, there are literary and colloquial differences. The language practices of conversation differ in many subtle ways from those used in formal writing. Unless one can assume that formal writing is in itself more desirable than good conversation, the language practices peculiar to conversation cannot be rated in comparison with those of formal writing. Each set of language practices is best in its own special sphere of use; one will necessarily differ from the other.

Fourth, there are social or class differences. . . . It is, of course, practically impossible to mark the limits of any social class in this country. It is even extremely difficult to describe the special characteristics of any such class because of the comparative ease with which one passes from one social group to another, especially in youth, and the consequent mixture of group habits among those so moving. . . .

Just as the general social habits of such separated social groups naturally show marked differences, so their language practices inevitably vary. . . . In fact, part of the significance of the social differences in language habits can well be illustrated by a comparison with clothes. . . . A dress suit suggests an evening party (or in some places a hotel waiter); overalls suggest a piece of dirty work or possibly a summer camp. In like manner language forms and constructions not only fulfill a primary function of communicating meaning; they also suggest the circumstances in which those particular forms and constructions are usually employed.[1]

[1] Charles Carpenter Fries, *American English Grammar* (New York: Appleton-Century-Crofts, Inc., 1940), pp. 6-11. Copyright 1940, by the National Council of Teachers of English and Charles C. Fries. These and subsequent passages are reprinted by permission of Appleton-Century-Crofts, Inc.

It must also be acknowledged that standard language is a key that will open many doors, and, conversely, many doors may be closed to those with non-standard language. There is truth in the saying, "As you speak, so you are."

With our facilities of communication and transportation today, the life around us to which we must adjust, in reference to language, means not just one neighborhood, but our whole English-speaking community. To be secure in language, we need the comfort of knowing that we are not too extreme in our use of it. For complete security, our familiar language patterns ought not to be solely those of one small group, but rather ones that will fit into the patterns of usage generally accepted by most people. They should not contain major structural variations which stand out as extreme and which will limit acceptance to just the smaller group with which we intimately communicate. That there will be variations in group speech patterns and individuals is, as Fries indicates, inevitable, because groups tend to develop common characteristics and because people vary their speech as situations vary. Speech, then, functions on many different levels. However, for greatest happiness, we need the security of knowing that, as a basic tool, the language we use and the variations, or levels of it that we command so that we may be socially mobile, will serve us well in all areas of this country and among all English-speaking people.

It is to this varying, living, and growing set of language patterns which will serve us well that we apply the word "standard." Although there are certain accepted and, in many cases, pleasing differences that characterize the speech of various areas—New England, the South, and the Middle West—we do have in the United States, as Fries describes it:

> a set of language habits, broadly conceived, in which the major matters of the political, social, economic, educational, religious life of this country are carried on. To these language habits is attached a certain social prestige, for the use of them suggests that one has constant relations with those who are responsible for

the important affairs of our communities. It is this set of language habits, derived originally from an older London English, but differentiated from it somewhat by its independent development in this country, which is the "standard" not because it is any more correct or more beautiful or more capable than other varieties of English; it is "standard" solely because it is the particular type of English which is used in the conduct of the important affairs of our people. It is also the type of English used by the *socially acceptable* of most of our communities, and insofar as that is true it has become social or class dialect in the United States.[2]

The obligation of teaching language in its standard varieties as a tool whereby economic and social security may be achieved has been taken on by the schools. As Fries goes on to say:

> Long have we in our national life adhered to the principle that no individual in his attempts to rise to the highest position should be disqualified by artificial restraints. Our people have been devoted to education because education has furnished the most important tool of social advancement. Our public schools have therefore held to the ideal that every boy and girl should be so equipped that he shall not be handicapped in his struggle for social progress and recognition and that he may rise to the highest positions. In the matter of the English language it is clear that any one who cannot use the language habits in which the major affairs of the country are conducted, the language habits of the socially acceptable of most of our communities, would have a serious handicap. The schools, therefore, have assumed the burden of training every boy and girl, no matter what his original social background and native speech, to use this "standard" English, this particular social or class dialect. To some pupils it is almost a foreign language; to others it is their accustomed speech. Many believe that the schools have thus assumed an impossible task.[3]

Fries points out that it may be the methods of procedure that are at fault and that school authorities may have directed their energies to teaching a make-believe correctness rather than that which is realisticially now standard.

[2] *Ibid.*, p. 13.

[3] *Ibid.*, p. 14.

Determining what are good standards in our language and then kindling a love and respect for them are joys that should be shared by all teachers and even all English-speaking adults. But this task is the special trust of the English teacher. Those English teachers, if there are any, who question this trust, who see little joy in it, who feel that the task may be useless and hopeless in some situations, we could ask not just, " Then, why teach English? " but, " Why teach? "

Assuming that the English teacher has clearly and realistically in mind the standard varieties of speech acceptable in his area and conscientiously takes on his share of the task of turning out graduates equipped to attain social and economic security in that area, the problem he faces may truly be a challenge. Because of the rapid migration of workers from rural Southern areas to Northern industrial cities where they have come for social and economic betterment, he may find in his classroom, as I did in Detroit, a great many students, particularly Negro students of a low socio-economic level, who habitually use a pattern of speech containing so many non-standard usages, reflecting all four types of speech differences, that their language seems unacceptable as good high-school-level speech in the new area. The pattern of speech may not only hinder the users socially and vocationally, but may give a false impression of ignorance and lend support to prejudice.

How can the high school English teacher best help these students overcome this disadvantage? How can he best go about teaching them standard English? How can he best point out the unacceptable speech differences without offending? How can the teacher help to eliminate a factor contributing to prejudice without appearing to be prejudiced? This is the problem that, I believe, has become a crisis in education today.

2 *Sensing The Problem*

In the midst of a trend toward taking a broader view of language in its multiplicity of aspects, I have chosen to move, seemingly, in the opposite direction. I am attempting to focus interest on one narrow channel to the specific language problem as I search for practical techniques that will be more effective in my specific language-teaching situation. While the general movement is toward climbing the ivory tower to get a good look at what language is and how it works, and thus to direct attention away from the many differences that exist in various speech communities, I am on the way down to try to make more effective application of what has been learned to a situation where language teaching is urgently needed, and, in most cases, just as urgently wanted.

Since the high-school teacher is engaged in the *doing*, his job is to meet the needs of his students, not by rationalizing their problems but by meeting them squarely with some program that will offer solutions. He knows the causes but must deal mainly with the symptoms.

That this specific language problem is a narrow channel in the light of all that is known about language cannot be disputed. It involves a comparatively small group of people whose problems seem large and real because they happen to be our students. It involves generalizing, even though one is concerned about specific users and specific speech forms. It involves criticism of an individual's language, a very personal possession. It suggests change. It says one level of usage is better than another because it is more generally acceptable. It honors the fact that our language is acceptable because we were lucky enough to be born in the Midwest, and Midwestern dialect in its standard form fortunately is one of the most widely used and most acceptable varieties of English in the United States. It implies to many of our students that we were born into a different social, economic, and cultural level than they and that they must change if they wish to fit into the general cultural pattern of our particular area. In other words, if they wish to progress in Northern and Midwestern urban communities, they must speak as we do. Surely this viewpoint *is* coming down from an ivory tower and is a narrow channel, but these are the facts the majority of our students face.

Our problem, although narrow in many respects, may have a wider scope in that it represents the problem of migrant people everywhere adjusting to the language pattern of their new community. Specifically, in a high school consisting predominantly of Negro students of a low socio-economic level in Detroit, it is concerned with how to change their patterns of speech which contain so many non-standard expressions that they are at a disadvantage socially and vocationally. They exist on an island of speech that tends to set them apart as a group, working against their social and economic progress, the purpose for which so many of their families came to Detroit.

Islands of speech keep people out of tune with the natural cultural changes that a living language constantly undergoes. It is precisely because language is in a constant state of change that many of the non-standard expressions used are now antiquated and ungrammatical in structure. They may be derived from African or Old English in the normal processes that bring about historical differences in speech. There are, however, no racial, biological, or physical reasons for Negro students to speak differently from white students.

In an article entitled, "The Relationship of the Speech of American Negroes to the Speech of Whites," Raven I. McDavid, Jr., and Virginia Glenn McDavid tell us:

Almost without exception, any scholar studying American Negro speech, whether as an end in itself or as part of a larger project, must dispose of two widely held superstitions: (1) he must indicate that there is no speech form identifiable as of Negro origin solely on the basis of physical characteristics; (2) he must show that it is probable that some speech forms of Negroes—and even of some whites—may be derived from an African cultural background by the normal processes of cultural transmission.[1]

George Philip Krapp wrote that

> Many of the characteristics of Negro English which are assumed to be the peculiar properties of the Negroes are merely archaic survivals of good old English. Such survivals might reasonably be expected, for a people more or less isolated from the central developments in the life of a race always retain cultural characteristics that the main body loses. This isolation may be geographical, like that of the Tennessee mountaineers, or it may be social, as with the Negroes.[2]

One needs only to look at the population figures to gain some insight into the social aspects of the problem. The rapid expansion of the automobile and allied industries attracted a sudden and continued migration of workers, both white and Negro, to the Detroit area. They came, and are still coming, from all parts of the country, but especially from the South. T. J. Woofter stated in 1933 that as soon as immigration was restricted, the vacuum thus created drew hundreds of thousands of Southern Negroes to the cities, and shifted 20 per cent of the Negro children of school age in the South to city schools.[3]

A few of our present Negro families date back to about 1810 when the census showed that there were 113 Negroes in Detroit, 96 free, and 17 slave. By 1900 there were 4,111 Negroes out of

[1] Raven I. McDavid, Jr., and Virginia Glenn McDavid, "The Relationship of the Speech of American Negroes to the Speech of Whites," *American Speech*, XXVI, No. 1 (1951), 3.

[2] George Philip Krapp, "The English of the Negro," *The American Mercury*, II (1924), 190.

[3] Thomas Jackson Woofter, Jr., *Races and Ethnic Groups in American Life* (New York: McGraw-Hill Book Co., 1933).

a total population of 285,704.[4] The increase in Negro population was gradual until 1910, when the number recorded in the *Thirteenth Census of the United States was* 5,741. Then the industrial rise came, which attracted over 35,000 Negroes to Detroit within ten years. This was followed by a boom of materials production, which brought over 79,000 Negroes, among others, to Detroit between the years 1920 and 1930. The rate of increase declined during the depression years, between 1930 and 1940, when around 29,000 Negroes arrived, to produce a total of 149,119 in 1940; but since that time the increase has been enormous. In the decade between 1940 and 1950, nearly 150,000 Negroes moved to Detroit. The Census total in 1950 was 298,875 out of a Detroit city population of 1,846,660.[5] As of July 1, 1957, Detroit stands as the fifth largest city in the United States with a total population of 1,910,000.[6] Of this, approximately 475,000, or more than 24 per cent are Negroes.[7]

Although both Negroes and whites bring to Detroit similar characteristics of speech, the whites, because they have entree to city white society on all of its various cultural levels, tend to be more readily assimilated and may sooner drop unusual characteristics of speech.[8] Many Negroes, forced into crowded areas, and perhaps preferring their " city-within-a city," in many cases are simply transported from a Southern neighborhood to a Northern one with no greater contact with white people and with very little contact with cultured Negroes.[9]

[4] Ulysses W. Boykin, *A Hand Book on the Detroit Negro* (Detroit: The Minority Study Associates, 1943), p. 17.

[5] U. S. Department of Commerce, Bureau of the Census, Thirteenth, Fifteenth, Sixteenth and Seventeenth Censuses of the U. S., volumes on *Population.*

[6] *Population, Housing and Economic Characteristics of the Detroit Standard Metropolitan Area 1957* (Detroit: *The Detroit News,* 1958).

[7] *The 5th Quinquennial Survey of the Detroit Market* (Detroit: *The Detroit News,* 1957), p. 10.

[8] Dr. Allison Davis, interview, May 11, 1956.

[9] Roi Ottley, " Mass Migration of Negroes from Rural Areas of the South to Industrial Centers in the North," a series in the *Detroit Free Press,* beginning May 27, 1956, and ending June 8, 1956.

It is no small wonder that the speech of many second or third generation Detroit Negroes may sound strange to Midwesterners of both races, although it was originally acceptable to some groups in the South. That their speech pattern has served these Negroes as a satisfactory means of communication among themselves is evidenced by the surprisingly excellent progress they have made in solving their own social and economic problems through their clubs, churches, and various social and cultural organizations.[10]

The Supreme Court decision of May 17, 1954, eliminating segregation in schools, caused no change in Detroit, for Detroit schools have been traditionally integrated. But little progress toward assimilation has been made in housing despite the Supreme Court decision of 1948 regarding the purchase of real property. During the last five years, the building of expressways, which cut through slum areas, has caused a dispersement of some Negro families into formerly all-white sections; but housing is still largely on the solid, rather than mixed, neighborhood plan. Even though students may attend any school within their home district, five of Detroit's high schools are predominantly Negro.

When I began this study, I had taught for twelve years in three of these Detroit schools, and prior to that, twelve years in other Michigan schools where I had no contact with Negro children or with others who used the same types of non-standard expressions. The unacceptable expressions used in speaking and writing by some of the students in these Michigan schools were of a general mixture of linguistic categories familiar to English teachers everywhere: *ain't, I seen, I done, have ran, have came, this here, that there, would of,* and *you was.* In my first teaching experience in Detroit, I had difficulty understanding many of the pupils during the first few days, for, added to the above locutions were many strange ones. Subsequently, some of my college students doing practice teaching have also

[10] A. M. Smith, "Negro Life in Detroit," *The Detroit News,* January 29, 1946.

needed a few days of adjustment to the differences in speech patterns.

Working closely with the better students in journalism activities, I observed how difficult it is for many students to develop standard speech, when they are so completely surrounded by different patterns. It was also apparent that many students who can speak well in class are not sufficiently motivated to continue speaking in an acceptable informal pattern, but often revert to substandard as soon as they leave the classroom. A walk through the corridors between classes with my ears attuned to the conversations at lockers brought this home forcefully.

After being promoted to department head, I found that conversations with people other than educators took on new meaning. For example, there was an attorney who complained, " When I go into a shoe-shine parlor and two of the boys are talking, I don't understand what they are saying. They're probably high school boys, too, or even graduates."

An engineer asked, " Why it is that all of my men are high school graduates, and all of them were born in Detroit, but when they're working together, they speak a different language? " We discussed such things as levels of language and compensation for injustices through sharing a comfortable common language. In defense of our schools, I stated that if they were high-school graduates, they knew how to speak well even if they didn't practice it. He replied, " I'm interested because I am one of the first engineers to place Negroes in responsible jobs paying $3.17 an hour. If they know better, I'm going to tell them that as long as they work for me, they must speak standard English."

These were practical cases where our high-school graduates, many of a low economic level, were being judged by middle-class Midwestern standards and were found lacking in speech proficiency. As a department head, I felt personally responsible and determined to seek effective ways of helping them. The pattern of non-standard expressions still used by so many high-school students gives a false impression of ignorance, and as with these two intelligent men, lends support to prejudice.

That non-standard speech may lend support to prejudice is discussed by Gunnar Myrdal, who is probably the greatest authority one can cite concerning problems relating to our students. He devotes a chapter to " 'Peculiarities' of Negro Culture and Personality," in which he states,

> We shall start from our conclusion in Chapter 6 that these differences have no basis in biological heredity, that they are of a purely cultural nature. . . . We shall try to take account of the diversity, but we feel we are justified in writing of Negro culture traits because *average* Negro behavior differs from *average* white behavior. From a practical standpoint it is necessary to take account of these differences in averages because white people see them and use them to buttress their prejudices.[11]
>
> To the Northern white man, although seldom to the Southern white man, the speech of the Negro seems unusual. In fact, the "Negro dialect" is an important cause of the Northern whites' unconscious assumption that Negroes are of a different biological type from themselves. . . . There is absolutely no biological basis for it; Negroes are as capable of pronouncing English words perfectly as whites are.
>
> Northern whites are also unaware of the reasons why they practically never hear a Negro speaking perfect English: First, at least three-fifths of the Negroes living in the North are Southern-born, and Negroes tend to retain the accent of their childhood, just as others do. Second, even most Northern-born Negroes were brought up in households and communities where they heard nothing but "Negro dialect" spoken. School was the only place to learn good English, and many Negroes did not, or could not, take adequate advantage of it. Third, Negroes seem to be proud of their dialect, and frequently speak it even when they know how to speak perfect English. Some upper class Negroes do this to retain prestige and a following among lower class Negroes. In the South a few educated Negroes do it to avoid appearing "uppity" in the eyes of the whites. Few Negroes seem to realize that the use of the dialect augments white prejudice, at least in

[11] Gunnar Myrdal, Richard Sterner and Arnold Rose, *An American Dilemma* (New York: Harper and Brothers, 1944), II, 956. This and subsequent passages are quoted with the permission of Harper and Brothers.

> the North. Fourth, most of those who know how to speak perfect English are members of the upper class, and these are so segregated that a large proportion of the whites can go through their entire lives without hearing one of them speak.
>
> As more Negroes become educated and urbanized, it may be expected that they will lose their distinctive cultural traits and take over the dominant American patterns.[12]

That poor speech may hinder our students socially is borne out by many studies which show the relationships between linguistic and social development. Helena Mallay has shown that as the child learns to make vocalized rather than motor approaches to other children, his socialization is facilitated.[13] Bernadine G. Schmidt states, " In fact, some authorities go so far as to say that the degree of the ability to use language is so closely related to the degree of social development that the measure of the language skill of a people is the measure of their civilization." [14] She has shown that speech therapy given to a group of mentally retarded girls facilitated their social development. Irene P. Davis reports " a positive correlation between maturity of articulation and acceptable social behavior." She states that " this may indicate either that the factors which retard a child's speech also retard his social development, or that a speech difficulty may contribute to social retardation." [15] Likewise, as our students continue to use non-standard, regional characteristics of speech, they may be retarded socially and thus vocationally.

The problem is heightened by the fact that these Negroes have come here hoping to progress socially and economically. They depend on the schools to effect the necessary changes.

[12] *Ibid.*, pp. 965-966.

[13] Helena Mallay, "A Study of Some of the Techniques Underlining the Establishment of Successful Social Contacts at the Preschool Level," *Journal of Genetic Psychology*, XLVII (1935), 431.

[14] Bernadine G. Schmidt, " Language Development as an Aid to the Social Adjustment of Mental Defectives," *Mental Hygiene,* XXV (1941), 402 ff.

[15] Irene P. Davis, " The Speech Aspects of Reading Readiness," *Newer Practices in Reading in the Elementary School, Seventeenth Yearbook. Bulletin of the Department of Elementary School Principals,* N. E. A. (Washington, National Education Association, 1938), p. 286.

M. A. Hawkins, who made a classic study of the dilemma of secondary education for Negroes, states that " compared to the occupation of parents, who were principally unskilled workers, the occupational choices of students were highly weighted in the direction of ' white-collar ' occupations." [16] Yet, his study shows that more than a third of the graduates in Baltimore he examined entered unskilled work.

Horace M. Bond states:

> All studies have shown that while the occupational distribution of Negro high-school graduates is on levels generally higher than that of the race as a whole, there is a wide discrepancy between expressed choice and actual occupation. Of 1,452 North Carolina high-school graduates, only 26.9 per cent went to college.[17]

He lists six studies (by E. A. Dimmick, R. W. Bullock, Charles Hyte, E. A. Mebane, D. A. Wilkerson, W. H. Gray, Jr.) which show that Negro secondary-school students generally list the professions among their occupational choices.

I believe that the lack of speech proficiency is a contributing cause of the failure of many Negro students to enter college, the first step toward achieving their occupational goals. I also believe that the resulting frustration surely does not contribute to better human relations.

Vocational retardation is tied in with the fact that non-standard speech gives a false impression of ignorance. When our students during the tension of an oral interview revert to their early language habits, the assumption is that if they learned no more about language usage during the four years of high school than they exhibit, then they probably learned little about anything else. Actually, they may be very capable in other respects but may simply have been satisfied with the familiar rather than the more cultured usage to convey their

[16] Horace M. Bond, " Negro Education," in Walter S. Monroe, Ed., *Encyclopedia of Educational Research* (Rev. ed., New York: Macmillan Co., 1950), p. 784.

[17] *Ibid.*, p. 785.

meaning. They are unaware of their habitual differences in speech pattern and the extent to which they are judged by them.

Further, judgments concerning intelligence are often based on reading ability. Mildred A. Dawson, a member of the Committee of the National Conference on Research in English, quotes Gertrude Hildreth, Gertrude Whipple, and other educators in the field of reading in pointing out the relationship between linguistic ability and reading achievement. Miss Hildreth, as early as 1949, remarked that " case studies have proven retardation in language to be a common accompaniment if not direct cause of reading failures " and that " [Miss] Whipple, in considering remedial programs in relation to basic programs of reading, said that one of many contributing causes of reading deficiency among 83 pupils who had been studied intensively was inferior language equipment." [18] Miss Dawson summarizes by stating that " throughout the program of reading instruction, a child's language usage defines his potential for learning to read and sets the limits of his proficiency as a reader." [19]

Dorothea McCarthy states,

> There is abundant evidence in the literature to show that children from the upper socio-economic groups are more advanced in all aspects of language development. Since intelligence is usually measured by means of verbal tests, it is difficult or impossible from available data to say whether these differences are due to differences in intellectual capacity, or whether the differences in intelligence-test scores merely reflect more basic differences in language development.[20]

She cites studies by Edith A. Davis, Dorothea McCarthy, Ella J. Day, and Florence M. Young in support.

Three Negro educators called my attention to the relation-

[18] Mildred A. Dawson, " Interrelationships Between Speech and Other Language Arts Areas," *Interrelationships Among the Language Arts* (Champaign, Ill.: The National Council of Teachers of English, [1954]), pp. 29, 30.

[19] *Ibid.*, p. 31.

[20] Dorothea McCarthy, " Child Development: Language," in Walter S. Monroe, Ed., *op. cit.*, p. 170.

ship between speech, reading, and mental testing. They were Dr. Allison Davis, of the University of Chicago, outstanding authority on Negro problems; Dr. Harold Harrison, Principal of Miller Junior High School, Detroit; and Dr. Nathaniel P. Tillman, Dean of the Graduate School, Atlanta University. Tillman mentioned that " in a state neighboring Georgia," a statewide test a few years ago indicated that Negro students in the eighth grade were reading on the fifth grade level and that in Georgia the students in the last semester of the twelfth grade showed an average of seventh grade reading level. Obviously, they would have difficulty understanding the vocabulary used in mental tests based on reading. Davis and Robert Hess remark: " The evidence that standard tests, now used in schools, are inadequate to fully diagnose *real* mental ability was clear after an intensive and cooperative three-year study at the University of Chicago." [21]

What do such tests show? *The National Survey of the Higher Education of Negroes* in analyzing the characteristics of high-school seniors as prospective college material sets forth the lack of preparation for college work as the greatest problem. This is said to be supported by relatively low scores on a test of mental ability in which Northern high-school seniors tested slightly below national norms, urban Southern students considerably below, and rural students far below acceptable norms.[22]

The fact that speech is related to reading and that mental tests are largely based on reading comprehension bears out the statement that non-standard speech may give a false impression of ignorance. If we concentrate on speech improvement and encourage reading for the purpose of enriching thought for speech, future statistics on the mental ability of seniors in the Northern area may show a better and truer picture.

[21] Allison Davis and Robert D. Hess, "What About IQ's?" *National Education Association Journal*, XXXVIII (1949), 604.

[22] F. J. Kelly, Director, *National Survey of the Higher Education of Negroes, General Studies of Colleges for Negroes,* Misc. No. 6, Vol. II (Washington: Office of Education, 1942), Chapter 4.

3 *Defining The Problem*

As a citizen, I am deeply interested in the total problem of bringing about better understanding among races. In our Northern industrial-city high schools, Negro students, many of low economic level, are judged by middle-class Caucasian standards. We need to find the educational practices and procedures that will bridge the gap and resolve differences.

As a teacher, critic, and head of an English department, my specific interest is how we can best promote common levels of standard, informal, American language. Non-standard expressions, which may be acceptable and used by both races in certain situations in other areas, I believe, are not acceptable in Midwestern areas. White migrants, because of the comparative ease of social, vocational, and even economic adjustments, tend to conform to new language patterns, but a great many Negroes, largely because of segregated housing, tend to retain group characteristics of speech. In many cases, differences in speech, which are reflected in writing, are so pronounced that many Negro students may be said to use a "second language," to which they revert as soon as they are out of the classroom.

This second language, mainly of good English origin but now containing archaic expressions which are said to have been leveled out of American white speech,[1] is characterized by an almost complete reversal of the standard practice of agreement in number between the subject and the verb; e. g., *he do, she have, they is.* Other verb troubles involve omission of the

[1] George Philip Krapp, "The English of the Negro," *American Mercury,* II (1924), 191.

auxiliary and confusion of tenses.[2] Many students may be said to add the sound of the letter *s* to a word, as in the pronoun *mine* (*mines*), and to leave it off where it belongs, as in *ten cents* (*ten cent*).[3] There is also excessive use of *be*, as in the expression *He don't be here.* Thus, besides the frequent substitution of the sound of *d* for *th* at the beginning, and that of *f* for *th* at the end of words and substitutions of the vowel *a* for the diphthong *i* to make *right* sound like *rat*, most of these language difficulties are grammatical. There is also an excessive rise in pitch which some authorities believe to be the key to pattern change.[4]

In his chapter entitled, "Which American Dialect is Best—For You?" James F. Bender tells us:

> There are of course a great many American and English dialects. We usually think of our native accents in three groups. These are: (a) *Eastern,* (b) *Midwestern,* or *General American,* and (c) *Southern.* The three are families; they have sub-divisions—no one knows exactly how many.
>
> The Southern family includes *Virginia Tidewater, General Lowland,* and *Southern Hill.* Listen to men like Harry S. Byrd of Virginia, Randolph Scott, Tom Connally of Texas, James S. Byrnes of South Carolina, and Kay Kyser as examples. Southern also includes the less populous *Cajun, Creole, Bayou,* and others. How many in all? At least a baker's dozen is a fair guess.
>
> In 1620 the first boatload of slaves arrived in Jamestown, Virginia, to work the large plantations laid out before the Pilgrims landed in New England.
>
> Southern culture of the time was indebted to France as much as to England. (You will recall that the Louisiana Territory still belonged to France in 1800.) You heard French almost as often as English. In 1736, Charleston had two theatres, one of them in French. Half the population spoke *la belle langue.* Many early

---

[2] Elmer Bagby Atwood, *A Survey of Verb Forms in the Eastern United States* (Ann Arbor: University of Michigan Press, 1953).

[3] "We have here almost certainly an analogical extension of the [-z] of *yours* and *ours* in absolute position. . . ." "Likewise with *cent.* There . . . is again an analogical form, the analogy being with the old uninflected genitive after numerals (cf. common *ten foot wide,* etc.)."—Letter of Harold B. Allen, January 26, 1958.

[4] Charles Hoffman, interview, April 23, 1956.

> records of Virginia and Maryland were written in French. This was the language of the cultivated homes and the great plantations.
>
> Charles II, the Merry Monarch, and his court also influenced the tastes of the South. This king, after a long exile in France, introduced *won't* as a contraction for *will not, wan't* for *was not* and *were not*. Charles set the style of using *ain't* for *amn't* and *aren't*. But only the illiterates said *ain't* instead of *is not, has not*, or *have not*.
>
> The slaves learned an English dialect with a heavy French savor. They dropped consonants at the ends of words. They brought to their new language deep and throaty voices—the result of large resonating chambers. The Negroes spoke and sang in languorous tempo. The slave women looked after the planters' children and thus became the mothers of the dialects we now call *Southern*.
>
> Southern dialects today strike your ear with characteristic intonation patterns. A Southerner breaks up, or "fractures," his vowels so that each one becomes two vowels, or a diphthong. He says '*ya-es*' for *yes*. He often drops word endings, especially consonants, as '*chile*' for *child*. In the same regions *penny* becomes '*pinny*,' etc. About twenty-two million Americans speak Southern dialects.[5]

We do not wish to change pleasing characteristics of Southern speech, such as the dropping of the final *r* and the quality that is generally called "softness" of speech, or other qualities which make the speech of the above-named nationally-known persons interesting as well as acceptable. Dialect enthusiasts, who study vowel enunciation, tell us that these pleasing qualities of Southern speech are moving northward into general acceptance.[6] Our concern is with non-standard, grammatical peculiarities which cause negative reactions in informal, as well as formal, cultural situations.

Present methods of language teaching are apparently not sufficiently adequate to help most of the students overcome

[5] James F. Bender, *How To Talk Well* (New York: McGraw-Hill Book Company, Inc., 1949), pp. 103-104. Copyright, 1949 by James F. Bender; quoted with permission of the publisher.

[6] Harold Whitehall, "American Dialects," speech before the Detroit English Club, April 21, 1955.

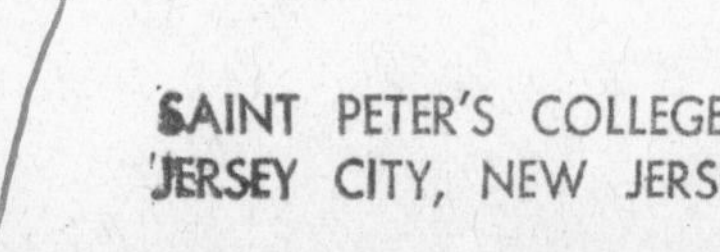

deep-rooted habits. We need to try new techniques for improving oral speech patterns. We have not been obtaining satisfactory results, and we apparently have not been completely successful in motivating improvement.

So that we might gain greater insight through a study of background factors and might learn the frequency of the use of specific language expressions, I prepared and administered a questionnaire to over 1200 upper-level high-school students in two distinct groups of schools: three predominantly Negro in population and three predominantly white. It was also given to 50 adults who had knowledge of the problem. The results of the adult responses are not included in this report except where they have contributed to our understanding.

The questionnaire was designed to reveal and clarify the nature of the problem and to discover what factors are most helpful in making students want to improve speech and what teaching techniques students think are most effective. It requested two separate listings of titles of books, plays, films and film strips, radio and television programs which the students think are helpful in improving speech and in helping people to get along better together.

The main part consisted of a check list of 102 non-standard expressions which the students were asked to check under three possible responses: I—those they might hear every day, II—those they have heard high-school graduates use, and III—those they themselves might use. Expressions unfamiliar to them were to be left unchecked.

The questionnaire did not provide commonly accepted expressions on the check list because these would have consumed too much time and space. It was designed to discover the admitted frequency of hearing and using unacceptable forms so that differences in patterns of speech could be indicated and so that objectionable forms eventually, if not eliminated, at least would be made less frequently. The students had freedom of choice to check or not to check.

One of the purposes of the questionnaire was to bring about

awareness that differences do exist, a fact not readily accepted by some persons whose ears may be so attuned to their particular way of speaking that they do not hear differences. The questionnaire has helped to stimulate awareness.

The findings should have far-reaching effects, for one of the first steps to correction is detection. My method of procedure is supported by Knight Dunlap's "Theory of Negative Practice," which involves the principle of bringing to conscious level the habits usually performed unconsciously.[7]

The findings should be generally useful to English teachers and textbook writers, especially the motivational factors, the teaching techniques, and the establishing of purposes and the changing of values. Those concerned with the language problems of many Negro students who may use non-standard, regional speech, or those concerned with changing any language patterns, will be interested in learning which expressions are most frequently heard and used by the two comparative groups and what the relationships of certain factors to certain expressions are. This knowledge should lead to the initiation of practice exercises and games to strengthen the use of standard forms.

As far as is known, this study is unique in scope and form. Other studies which remotely resemble this one are that made by Charters and Miller based on the grammatical errors of school chidren in Kansas City in 1915,[8] the Sterling Andrus Leonard study of 1932,[9] and the current studies being conducted for the Linguistic Atlas of the United States and Canada.[10] The Leonard study is the first attempt of any mag-

[7] Knight Dunlap, *Personal Adjustment* (New York: McGraw-Hill Book Company, 1946), p. 191.

[8] W. W. Charters and Edith Miller, "A Course of Study in Grammar Based upon the Grammatical Errors of School Children in Kansas City, Missouri," *University of Missouri Bulletin*, Education Series No. 9, XVI, No. 2 (1915), cited in H. A. Greene, "English–Language, Grammar, and Composition," in Walter S. Monroe, Ed., *op. cit.*, p. 390.

[9] Sterling A. Leonard, *Current English Usage*, English Monograph No. 1 (Champaign, Illinois: National Council of Teachers of English, 1932).

[10] Harold B. Allen, "The Linguistic Atlases: Our New Resource," *The English Journal*, XLV, No. 4 (1956), 188-194,

nitude to secure contemporary opinions on 230 items of disputed usage, placed in sentences, and rated according to level of acceptability by qualified judges. The current studies for the Linguistic Atlas consists of recording in phonetic transcriptions, through interviews, the actual usage of a long list of language items by three groups of people in any given area.

Little seems to have been written on any phase of the particular speech problems of the low socio-economic level Negro besides the writings of Myrdal, Krapp, Atwood, and the McDavids. Others known to have articles touching upon the subject are Edgar P. Billups, Nathan Van Patten, and Hawner Cobbs.[11]

Paul Onica, a fellow-teacher at Northeastern High School, reported in his Master's thesis on his success in trying out various remedial techniques with our students. He learned that the greater percentage of students in his Northeastern High School composition classes wanted to receive training in oral composition more than in any other phase of English work.[12]

Hans Kurath analyzes the pronunciation and enunciation phases of particular Southern speech patterns.[13] Dan Burley [14] and the Hermans,[15] in separate writings, describe extreme characteristics of theatrical Negro speech. Gullah, the dialect spoken by Negro inhabitants of the Sea Islands and those along the coast of South Carolina and Georgia, is described by the Her-

[11] Edgar P. Billups, "Some Principles for the Representation of Negro Dialect in Fiction," *Texas Review*, VIII (1923), 99-123; Nathan Van Patten, "The Vocabulary of the American Negro as Set Forth in Contemporary Literature," *American Speech*, VII (1931), 24-31; Hawner Cobbs, "Negro Colloquialism in the Black Belt," *Alabama Review*, V (1952), 203-212.

[12] Paul G. Onica, "A Study of Certain Substandard English Usage Habits: Some Causes and Suggested Remedial Procedures" (Unpublished Master's thesis, Wayne State University, 1954), p. 7.

[13] Hans Kurath, Society for Pure English, Tract No. XXX, *American Pronunciation* (London: Clarendon Press, 1928), pp. 280-295.

[14] Dan Burley, *Original Handbook of Harlem Jive* (New York: published by the author, 1944).

[15] Lewis Helmar Herman and Marguerite Shalett Herman, *Manual of American Dialects for Radio, Stage and Screen* (Chicago: Ziff Davis Publishing Co., 1947), Chapter III.

mans, by Mason Crum, and by Lorenzo D. Turner.[16] John Dyneley Prince describes Surinam Negro-English.[17]

The words *speech* and *language* do not appear in the titles of 130 problems listed by D. A. Wilkerson in his article in the *Journal of Negro Education*. Problem I under " Problems of Education," however, is " the problem of reducing the disproportionate amount of illiteracy among Negroes, including both absolute and ' marginal ' illiteracy." [18]

To summarize the lack of research in the general field of remedial teaching, Leo J. Brueckner concludes his article, " Diagnosis in Teaching," in *The Encyclopedia of Educational Research*, thus:

> Relatively little is known concerning the precise types of remedial treatment that should be applied to most kinds of learning difficulties. This whole field merits extended research. There is no phase of educational method that is more seriously in need of study. The returns should be great.

The present study may help to supply some of this lack, provide the teacher with some remedial work in general, acquaint him with a particular problem of regional, archaic speech in the urban high schools and show him how to cope with it.

[16] L. H. and M. S. Herman, *op. cit.*, Chapter VI; Mason Crum, " Gullah; Negro Life in the Carolina Sea Islands," *Duke University Publications*, XV (Durham, N. Car.: Duke University Press, 1940) ; Lorenzo D. Turner, " Problems Confronting the Investigator of Gullah," *American Dialect Society Publications*, IX (1947) , 74-84.

[17] John Dyneley Prince, " Surinam Negro-English," *American Speech*, IX (1934) , 181-186.

[18] D. A. Wilkerson, " The Peculiar Problems of Negroes in American Social Life," *Journal of Negro Education*, V (1930) , 324.

4 *The Questionnaire and Its Results*

The questionnaire, called *Speech Improvement, A Key to Better Understanding,* was given to over 1200 eleventh and twelfth grade students in six Detroit high schools. Three of the schools have a population consisting predominantly of Negro students [1] and three predominantly of white students.[2] Unfortunately, due to an accident in transportation and storage, a box containing the total returns of one school disappeared and through circumstances beyond control are not available.[3] Since this school, one of predominantly white population, represented a higher socio-economic level than the others, with the exception of one which is rated equal,[4] the loss does not seriously affect the study.

The results given here are based on the complex returns from five schools, or a total of 902 student questionnaires. There were 680 in Group S, those schools with predominantly a Negro population (Southern); and 222 in Group D, those with predominantly a white population (Detroit).[5] Results are given in percentages of the respective groups.

I administered the questionnaire directly. By way of introduction, I asked the students, as upperclassmen, to assist in this effort to find better ways of helping others to improve their

[1] Northeastern High School, Miller High School, Northern High School.

[2] Denby High School, Cody High School, Cooley High School.

[3] Denby High School.

[4] Cooley High School; see rating in *Social Rating of Community Areas in Detroit* by United Community Services of Metropolitan Detroit Research Department (Detroit: United Community Services, 1955), pp. 4-7.

[5] No record of race is kept in the Detroit schools. Although speech differences are not biological, for those who object to the unscientific term "predominantly," I observed that there were 46 "apparently" white children in Group S and 2 "apparently" colored children in Group D.

speech.[6] A code number was used for each school, and individuals were not identified by their questionnaires.

Although the students were urged to be truthful, and students usually are, the tendency is to minimize the checking of non-standard expressions where these are generally recognized as familiar, especially when their use is admitted. On the other hand, where the pattern is generally unfamiliar, the tendency may be to check because of the desire to contribute. For this reason, the differences in the extent of familiarity with the speech pattern between the two groups may be actually much greater than the figures indicate.

The findings, however, show that all of the expressions listed are a part of the speech pattern heard and used by some students in Group S, and they are, on an average, both heard and used approximately four times as frequently by students in Group S as by those in Group D.

1. Number of Checks Per Expression, in Per Cent and in Relation to Group

	HEARD *Group*		GRADS. USE *Group*		YOU USE *Group*	
	S	D	S	D	S	D
Highest number of checks per expression	551	127	335	88	318	63
Lowest	89	0	23	1	7	0
Total number of checks	28,752	2,282	12,213	1,217	9,427	653
Average number of checks per expression	282	22	120	12	92	6
Percent average number is of group	41%	10%	18%	5%	14%	3%
Number in group	680	222	680	222	680	222

Number of expressions 102

[6] There were 644 twelfth grade students and 258 eleventh grade students in all, with approximately an equal proportion of each grade in each school.

Since these were upperclassmen only, of which 71 per cent were seniors, the picture this suggests for the high school as a whole, and the lower grades as well, presents a serious problem. Students of schools represented by Group S are surely at a disadvantage in this area when competing with students of Group D in any type of judgment based on what is probably the most important tool in life—speech.

Out of the 102 expressions, 30 were checked as ones " which you may hear every day " by 50 per cent to 81 per cent of the students in group S. There were 39 other expressions checked as " often heard " by one-third to one-half of the students in Group S. Only two expressions, *I done it*, and *It don't*, were checked by more than 50 per cent of the students in group D. Only three additional expressions, *Didn't have nothin'*, *I seen the pi'ture*, and *You was there*, were checked as " often heard " by one-third to one-half of the students in Group D. The contrast here is 30 to 2 and 39 to 3.

Table 2 lists the thirty expressions " often heard " by 50 per cent or more of the students in Group S. It shows the percentage of each group who checked the expressions in each of the three columns: Heard—*Which you may hear every day*; Graduates Use—*Which you have heard high-school graduates use*; and You Use—*Which you yourself may ever use.*

Of the expressions used in the questionnaire, Table 3 probably presents the ones most different from the general speech pattern of the Detroit area.

Some estimate of the comparative economic levels of the students tested may be gained from Tables 4 and 5, which show the occupations of the parents.

Because of the magnitude of the study, twelve expressions representing a sampling of the types of difficulties showing greatest differential between the two groups were chosen to test the relationships between the background factors and the expressions. These are presented in Tables 6, 7 and 8. The figures given show the percentage of students in each particular classification who checked the various expressions.

2. *Thirty Expressions* HEARD *by 1/2 or More of Group S., in Percentages*

EXPRESSIONS	HEARD *Group* S	D	GRADS. USE *Group* S	D	YOU USE *Group* S	D
I done it.	81	57	49	40	37	20
It don't.	75	56	48	40	46	29
You was there.	74	40	43	18	42	6
Didn't have nothin'.	71	45	34	25	25	16
Yes, you is!	71	20	33	6	30	5
Yes, it do!	70	11	37	7	39	1
I seen the pi'ture.	69	51	47	30	38	20
Thanks a lots.	68	25	39	15	43	15
She say—	65	15	31	5	23	1
I works hard.	63	12	27	4	25	2
I sung it.[a]	60	26	25	12	17	6
I have wrote.	60	25	37	20	27	8
You comin', ain't you?	60	19	23	10	19	6
Sometime I do.	59	28	35	16	46	17
It's fifty cent.	59	8	38	6	40	5
It sho' have.	58	15	24	6	17	5
Now you talkin'!	58	18	30	10	27	5
He have a—	58	8	31	5	29	2
That's mines.	58	2	28	1	30	1
He asked would I go.	55	19	31	15	33	9
He love to go.	55	8	26	3	23	1
We all knows that, man!	52	20	26	12	18	3
They have came.	52	15	25	12	20	6
He graduate last June.	52	10	37	7	24	2
Chunk the ball.	52	8	14	5	6	5
The boy have a dog.	52	5	26	1	28	1
That mean—	50	15	28	6	28	4
I likes things nice.	50	8	21	3	15	3
Those peoples—	50	5	19	3	13	1
Two mens—	50	2	19	1	11	1
Average of above	60	20	31	12	27	7

[a] Standard variant.

2. *Continued.*

Range in percentages of 39 expressions heard by 1/3 to 1/2 of students in Group S, in percentages

Highest	49	25	25	19	19	6
Lowest	34	1	8	1	4	0
Average	40	8	15	4	11	2

3. *Expressions Representing Greatest Differential in Percentages*

(Gained by subtracting the percentages of Group D from Group S)

	Differential in Per Cent		
EXPRESSIONS	HEARD	GRADS. USE	YOU USE
Yes, it do!	59	30	38
That's mines.	56	27	29
It's fifty cent.	51	32	35
Yes, you is!	51	27	27
I works hard.	51	23	23
She say—	50	26	22
He have a—	50	26	27
Two mens—	48	18	10
The boy have a dog.	47	25	28
He love to go.	47	23	23
Those peoples—	45	16	12
They likes to go.	45	14	14
Chunk the ball.	44	9	1
He taken her home.	43	22	18
It sho' have.	43	18	12
Thanks a lots.	43	24	28
Nice day, ain't?	43	10	10
He graduate last June.	42	30	22
I likes things nice.	42	18	12
He absent.	41	19	18
You comin,' ain't you?	41	13	13
Now you talkin'!	40	20	22
A lots a peoples—	39	17	12

3. Continued.

EXPRESSIONS	*Differential in Per Cent* HEARD	GRADS. USE	YOU USE
They pays my rent.	39	15	8
Y'all ain't listenin'.	39	9	7
I clean house yesterday.	37	13	13
She cry all night.	37	15	13
He asked would I go.	36	26	24
That make it nice.	36	17	16
They have came.	36	13	14
He carry her to church.	36	14	10
That mean—	35	22	24
I have wrote.	35	17	19
Isn't they?	35	16	13
We loves it.	35	13	14
You was there.	34	25	32
I sung it.[a]	34	13	11
She hope him.	34	10	6
They doesn't want to.	33	15	14
They writes letters.	33	13	11
I cleans good.	33	12	8
She stays by her auntie's.	33	10	8
They bofe gone.	33	10	6
What yo' mean, gal?	33	9	5
Like so many has done.	32	15	11
We all knows that, man!	32	14	15
They wears—	32	13	9
Sometime I do.	31	19	29
I plays golf.	31	15	8
We has enough.	31	11	11
They hits him.	31	12	10
How many womens there?	31	10	8
Unlessen—	31	9	6
That's his'n, honey chile.	31	5	3
He twenty-one.	30	11	11
Has you eat?	30	11	5

[a] Standard variant.

4. Occupational Status of Father, in Percentages

STATUS	*Group S*	*Group D*
Professional and educational	1	1
Managerial	1	11
Clerical and sales	1	6
Service	4	3
Skilled	10	48
Semi-skilled	48	23
Unskilled	4	2
Hospitalized or institutionalized	1	0
Unemployed	10	1
Deceased or divorced	5	3
Not known or rejects	16	3

5. Occupational Status of Mother, in Percentages

STATUS	*Group S*	*Group D*
Professional and educational	1	3
Managerial	1	1
Clerical and sales	1	5
Service	1	0
Skilled	3	12
Semi-skilled	10	10
Unskilled	4	1
Housewife (husband employed)	41	53
Hospitalized or institutionalized	0	0
Unemployed (no husband or husband unemployed)	16	2
Deceased or divorced	2	1
Not known or rejects	21	14

The tables show the relationships only for the S Group, since the statistics substantiate the fact that they are the ones who are the greatest hearers and users of the non-standard expressions and, therefore, need the most understanding and help.

In Tables 6, 7 and 8 the order of the expressions is changed to correspond with the order in which they appear in the questionnaire.

The percentages given in Table 6 show that, in general, as the economic level is lowered, the expressions are more frequently used. However, it is interesting to note that with *She say* this is not the case; and there are other slight variations with *Yes, you is!*

6. *Father's Occupation in S group in Relation to Checks in* YOU USE *Column*

In per cent of each classification who checked each expression

EXPRESSIONS SHOWING GREATEST DIFFERENTIAL	*Professional and educational Managerial*	*Clerical and sales Service Skilled*	*Semi-skilled Unskilled*	*Hospitalized or institutionalized Unemployed Deceased or divorced*
She say—	25	25	22	23
He have a—	8	28	28	34
Yes, it do!	25	37	42	40
Yes, you is!	33	24	29	34
I works hard.	8	14	27	25
He graduate last June.	8	19	23	26
He taken her home.	8	18	19	21
He absent.	8	20	17	21
Two mens—	0	12	10	12
Those peoples—	0	14	12	13
That's mines.	8	28	30	32
It's fifty cent.	25	43	40	41
Number of returns in each class	12	101	356	104

Total number of returns	573
Not known or rejects	107
Total in group	680

Table 7 shows that the expressions are admittedly heard by a comparatively consistent percentage regardless of economic status.

7. *Father's Occupation in S group in Relation to Checks in the* HEARD *Column*

In per cent of each classification who checked each expression

EXPRESSIONS SHOWING GREATEST DIFFERENTIAL	*Professional and educational Managerial*	*Clerical and sales Service Skilled*	*Semi-skilled Unskilled*	*Hospitalized or institutionalized Unemployed Deceased or divorced*
She say—	75	68	65	66
He have a—	67	64	55	62
Yes, it do!	75	65	72	69
Yes, you is!	75	73	70	75
I works hard.	42	61	65	65
He graduate last June.	50	53	52	48
He taken her home.	50	45	50	43
He absent.	50	47	47	47
Two mens—	50	47	52	47
Those peoples—	58	50	50	49
That's mines.	58	62	57	54
It's fifty cent.	67	64	58	60
Number of returns in each class	12	101	356	104

Total number of returns	573
Not known or rejects	107
Total in group	680

The occupational status of the mother shows a more positive relationship to the number of expressions checked than does the occupational status of the father.

8. *Mother's Occupational status in S Group in Relation to Checks in* HEARD *Column*

In per cent of each classification who checked each expression

EXPRESSIONS SHOWING GREATEST DIFFERENTIAL	*Professional and educational Managerial*	*Clerical and sales Service Skilled Unskilled*	*Housewife (husband employed)*	*Unemployed (no husband)*	*Deceased[a] or divorced*
She say—	45	64	68	61	75
He have a—	27	62	60	55	63
Yes, it do!	45	76	72	70	68
Yes, you is!	36	70	74	72	75
I works hard.	27	60	66	61	75
He graduate last June.	36	57	52	51	63
He taken her home.	27	48	48	49	63
He absent.	27	48	48	47	44
Two mens—	36	51	51	46	50
Those peoples—	36	54	54	45	56
That's mines.	27	61	60	56	63
It's fifty cent.	55	63	61	58	69
Number of returns in each class	11	127	280	106	16

Total number of returns	540
Not known or rejects	140
Total in group	680

[a] *There was none classified as hospitalized or institutionalized.*

As can be seen from the distribution in Table 9, slightly less than half of the students in Group S were born in Detroit and more than half of them started school in Detroit. Twenty-five per cent were born in Alabama, Georgia, and Mississippi, but only 15 per cent started school there.

9. Geographical Background of 680 in S Group in Percentages

LOCATION	Place where student was born Group		Place where student started school Group		One other place in family background Group	
	S	D	S	D	S	D
Detroit	45	71	63	82	—	—
Ala.	13	.4	8	.4	9	.4
Ga.	7	0	4	0	10	.4
Miss.	5	0	3	0	3	.4
Ky., Tenn., Mo.	6	3	4	2	9	5
Okla., Tex., Ark., N. Mex., Ariz.	5	0	3	0	5	2
Fla., La.	4	0	2	0	4	2
Ill., Ind., Ohio	4	3	3	1	14	10
Md., D. of C., Va., N. C., S. C.,	4	.4	3	0	4	1
N. Y., N. J., Penn., Del., W. Va.	2	4	2	2	8	19
Mich. (outside Detroit), Wis., Minn., Iowa	1	12.4	3	8	1	9
N. D., S. D., Mont., Wy., Ida., Neb., Kan., Colo., Utah	1	.4	1	.4	1	2
Wash., Ore., Cal., Nev.	1	.4	0	0	2	.4
Me., N. H., Ver., Mass., R. I., Conn.	0	1	0	.4	1	2
Another country	1	4	0	3	1	18
No answer	1	0	1	1	28	28

Table 10 shows the five top-ranking birthplaces in relation to the admitted use of the expressions and reveals that Detroit-born students use these expressions only slightly less than those born in the Deep South.

10. Place Where Student was Born in Relation to Expressions Used, in Percentages

EXPRESSIONS	Detroit	Ala.	Ga.	Miss.	Ky. Tenn. Mo.
She say—	21	25	29	29	27
He have a—	27	35	40	34	22
Yes, it do!	38	43	50	9	36
Yes, you is!	33	27	33	29	29
I works hard.	24	27	31	40	18
He graduate last June.	27	25	29	17	22
He taken her home.	20	21	19	26	11
He absent.	19	22	15	31	16
Two mens—	10	12	13	29	9
Those peoples—	11	13	15	20	16
That's mines.	29	33	40	49	31
It's fifty cent.	41	43	40	40	36
NUMBER OF STUDENTS	308	89	48	35	45

To the question, " By whom were you reared during your first five years when your speech pattern was being formed? " the answers, given here in percentages of the total checks for Groups S and D, were as follows:

11. Relative by Whom Students Were Reared, in Percentages

RELATIVE	*Group S*	*Group D*
Mother	85	94
Grandmother	10	5
Aunt	2	0
Sister	1	0
Some other person or persons	2	1

Twenty-eight students in Group S and six in Group D checked two each, probably to indicate that they were reared by both the mother and the grandmother.

Those reared by their mother both heard and used the expressions more frequently than those reared by some other person. Table 12 shows the average per cent for the twelve expressions used and heard by Group S.

12. Relationship of Expressions to Relative by Whom Reared, for S Group, in Average Percentages

HEARD		USED	
Mother	*Other*	*Mother*	*Other*
58	41	25	18

Answers to the question, " With whom did you live during your first five years? " might give some indication of the element of security felt by the child during these formative years. The percentages of the total number of checks for each group are as follows:

13. Relative with Whom Students Lived, in Percentages

RELATIVE	*Group S*	*Group D*
Both parents	71.0	92.0
Mother alone	11.0	4.0
Father alone	1.0	0.0
Father and step-mother	1.0	0.5
Mother and step-father	2.0	0.5
Grandparents	10.0	2.0
Other relatives	2.0	0.5
Guardians	1.0	0.0
Institution	1.0	0.5

Twenty students in Group S and two in Group D checked more than one.

A little variation in Group S occurred when the expressions often heard were compared with a factor indicating security. The breakdown was in three classifications as shown in Table 14. Only the highest and lowest figures and those for two other examples are given.

14. Relationship of Expressions HEARD *to Relative with Whom S Group (680) Students Lived, in Percentages*

EXPRESSIONS	*Both parents*	*Mother or father alone*	*Some other person*
Yes, you is! (highest)	69	73	69
He absent. (lowest)	45	48	47
Yes, it do!	68	70	75
That's mines.	56	65	56
NUMBER OF STUDENTS	487	82	111

To the question, " What is the highest school level completed by the person who reared you ? " the following answers for the mother, shown in percentages, were given.

15. Education of Mother, in Percentages

SCHOOL LEVEL COMPLETED	*Group S*	*Group D*
Grades 1 or 2	1	0
Grades 3 or 4	2	0
Grades 5 or 6	5	1
Grades 7 or 8	20	15
Grades 9 or 10	24	15
Grades 11 or 12	36	49
1 or 2 years of college	6	13
3 or 4 years of college	1	6
5 or more years of college	0	1
Rejects	5	0

As can be seen in Table 16, the number of expressions checked generally falls off as the education of the parent advances, shown from left to right in the three-column series. In a few expressions there is approximately a 20 per cent drop, but in one, *He graduate last June,* there is a 33 per cent increase in the " heard " column. The number of returns, 18, for grades 1-4, I recognize is small.

Answers to the question, " What is the highest school level completed by your father, or the man closest to you during your first five years? " are reported in Table 17. See also Table 18.

16. Education of Mother of S Group in Relation to Expressions HEARD *and* USED, *in Percentages*

	HEARD			USED		
EXPRESSIONS	*Grades* 1-4	*Grades* 5-12	*College* 1-5 yrs.	*Grades* 1-4	*Grades* 5-12	*College* 1-5 yrs.
She say–	72	63	74	22	23	23
He have a–	61	58	57	28	30	23
Yes, it do!	72	71	64	50	39	34
Yes, you is!	67	72	62	33	31	23
I works hard.	61	64	58	22	25	15
He graduate last June.	22	52	55	22	23	19
He taken her home.	56	48	45	6	19	15
He absent.	56	46	47	6	20	9
Two mens–	61	50	47	12	11	6
Those peoples–	61	51	42	28	13	8
That's mines.	72	58	51	28	31	19
It's fifty cent.	61	59	62	56	40	34
NUMBER OF RETURNS	18	575	53	18	575	53

Total number of returns	646
Not known or rejects	34
Total in group	680

17. Education of Father, in Percentages

SCHOOL LEVEL COMPLETED	*Group S*	*Group D*
Grades 1 or 2	2	1
Grades 3 or 4	5	4
Grades 5 or 6	9	16
Grades 7 or 8	19	15
Grades 9 or 10	20	38
Grades 11 or 12	26	14
1 or 2 years of college	6	5
3 or 4 years of college	2	5
5 or more years of college	1	0
Rejects	10	2

18. Education of Father of S Group in Relation to Expressions HEARD *and* USED, *in Percentages*

	HEARD			USED		
EXPRESSIONS	*Grades* 1-4	*Grades* 5-12	*College* 1-5 yrs.	*Grades* 1-4	*Grades* 5-12	*College* 1-5 yrs.
She say—	65	65	64	17	23	27
He have a—	63	58	54	28	31	16
Yes, it do!	72	71	64	63	38	34
Yes, you is!	73	71	64	43	30	25
I works hard.	70	66	51	33	25	20
He graduate last June.	41	53	46	15	24	18
He taken her home.	41	50	38	24	19	11
He absent.	50	46	51	17	19	16
Two mens—	63	62	50	13	11	7
Those peoples—	65	50	38	15	13	9
That's mines.	70	58	51	35	31	18
It's fifty cent.	57	61	54	48	41	25
NUMBER OF RETURNS	46	513	56	46	513	56

Total number of returns	615
Not known or rejects	65
Total in group	680

The questionnaire asked: "Check which of the following are brought regularly into your home for you to read if you wish: (You may check as many as five, or you may leave all blank if you don't have any of them.)" Table 19 shows the returns, in percentages.

19. Newspapers and Periodicals in the Home, in Percentages

READING MATERIAL	*Group S* (680)	*Group D* (222)
A daily newspaper	43	35
A weekly news magazine	15	21
A hobby or fiction magazine	7	11
A literary magazine	7	10
A humor magazine	8	5

Some other paper or magazine	19	18
Rejects (probably indicating none)	.4	0
NUMBER OF NEWSPAPERS OR PERIODICALS CHECKED		
Checked 1	30	13
Checked 2	30	29
Checked 3	24	32
Checked 4	11	15
Checked 5	4	10
Checked 6	1	1
Total number of checks	1552	632
Rejects	7	0
Grand total	1559	632

Table 19 shows that less than half of the students in both groups take a daily newspaper, but that 30 per cent in the S

20. Newspapers and Periodicals for S Group in Relation to Expressions HEARD *and* USED, *in Percentages*

EXPRESSION	HEARD *1 Only*	HEARD *3 or More*	USED *1 Only*	USED *3 or More*
She say–	66	67	30	20
He have a–	59	57	34	25
Yes, it do!	70	71	40	37
Yes, you is!	67	70	33	28
I works hard.	69	63	27	20
He graduate last June.	56	54	30	20
He taken her home.	53	49	19	19
He absent.	48	46	21	18
Two mens–	56	50	16	11
Those peoples–	56	50	19	11
That's mines.	60	59	33	28
It's fifty cent.	61	60	45	39
NUMBER OF RETURNS	200	267	200	267

Number of returns of 1 or 3 or more	467
Number of returns of 2	206
Not known or rejects	7
Total in S group	680

Group take two periodicals and 32 per cent in the D Group take three.

Negro publications, although not daily newspapers, may account for the greater number checked by the S Group.

Each of the above expressions is used less frequently by those who have more reading matter in the home. There is a positive relationship between the number of newspapers and periodicals brought into the home and better speech usage. See Table 20.

Table 21 shows the responses to: "Check the approximate number of books you have in your home library."

21. Books in Home Library, in Percentages

NUMBER OF BOOKS	*Group S*	*Group D*
0– 9	21	9
10–19	24	11
20–29	15	10
30–39	12	12
40–49	6	9
50 or more	16	48
Rejects	6	1

There is a definite relationship between the number of books in the home and the quality of speech. Those with more books used our dozen expressions less frequently. Reading background has definite bearing on speech usage. See Table 22.

The results of the question, "How often do you and your family attend religious services?" are shown in Table 23.

Nine out of twelve expressions shown in Table 24 were checked as "heard" by a greater percentage of those who attended religious services than by those who practically never attended.

Table 25 tabulates the answers in percentages for each group to the question, "Have you ever talked to a stranger on the telephone and by his way of speaking been able to picture him as belonging to a particular racial or nationality group?"

22. *Books in Home Library of S Group in Relation to Expressions* HEARD *and* USED, *in Percentages*

	HEARD			USED		
EXPRESSIONS	0-9	10-49	50 or more	0-9	10-49	50 or more
She say–	71	62	69	29	22	14
He have a–	62	55	58	33	28	21
Yes, it do!	72	68	77	43	39	31
Yes, you is!	71	70	70	31	30	26
I works hard.	66	65	61	25	27	16
He graduate last June.	58	52	49	25	25	16
He taken her home.	52	48	43	18	20	16
He absent.	45	46	53	17	19	21
Two mens–	54	47	54	12	12	5
Those peoples–	48	49	59	10	13	13
That's mines.	62	58	54	31	33	21
It's fifty cent.	60	58	63	43	40	13
NUMBER OF RETURNS	143	387	112	143	387	112

Total number of returns	642
Not known or rejects	38
Total in group	680

23. *Attendance at Religious Services, in Percentages*

ATTENDANCE	*Group S*	*Group D*
Never	3	6
Once a year	3	6
Three or four times a year	3	6
Six or eight times a year	2	4
Once a month	2	3
Twice a month	8	6
Usually once a week	55	52
Usually twice a week	15	10
Usually more often than twice a week	8	5
Rejects	1	2

24. Attendance at Religious Services of S Group in Relation to Expressions Heard, in Percentages

	ATTENDANCE		
EXPRESSIONS	*Practically never (or once a year)*	*Seldom (three times a year to twice a month)*	*Often (once a week to more than twice a week)*
She say—	59	61	66
He have a—	46	53	59
Yes, it do!	70	63	71
Yes, you is!	68	65	72
I works hard.	51	63	64
He graduate last June.	57	60	51
He taken her home.	38	47	49
He absent.	46	50	46
Two mens—	46	51	50
Those peoples—	43	52	50
That's mines.	54	55	59
It's fifty cent.	59	63	59
NUMBER OF RETURNS	37	104	535

Total number of returns	676
Not known or rejects	4
Total in group	680

25. Judgments as to Race or Nationality, in Percentages

REPLIES	*Group S*	*Group D*
Yes	85	86
No	14	14
Rejects	1	0

Table 26 tabulates the answers, in percentages, to the question, " In talking to a stranger on the telephone, do you sometimes form conclusions as to his ' learning '? "

26. Judgments as to Learning, in Percentages

REPLIES	*Group S*	*Group D*
Yes	80	85
No	19	15
Rejects	1	0

Table 27 covers the question, " Do you think these conclusions could sometimes be wrong? " (This question was at the top of the page giving instructions for checking the expressions and could have been overlooked.)

27. Accuracy of Judgments, in Percentages

REPLIES	*Group S*	*Group D*
Yes	85	93
No	7	2
Rejects	8	5

Following the list of expressions in the questionnaire, the following questions (numbers 64-66) were asked, and Tables 28-36 tabulate the answers in percentages.

" Do you believe that certain expressions like those you have just read help to identify persons with particular racial or nationality groups? "

28. Judgments as to Identity, in Percentages

REPLIES	*Group S*	*Group D*
Yes	76	94
No	20	6
Rejects	4	0

" Do you believe that people outside of a particular group might think that if a person has 'learning,' he will use the language teaching he gets in school and through good reading and listening? "

29. Judgments as to Intelligence, in Percentages

REPLIES	*Group S*	*Group D*
Yes	88	90
No	8	8
Rejects	4	2

" Do you think that people outside of the group might get a wrong idea about a person's 'learning' if they hear him use some of these expressions? "

30. Judgments as to False Impressions, in Percentages

REPLIES	*Group S*	*Group D*
Yes	91	91
No	5	9
Rejects	4	0

" Do you think the use of such expressions could keep a person from being accepted into other social groups? "

31. Judgments as to Social Disadvantages, in Percentages

REPLIES	*Group S*	*Group D*
Yes	85	85
No	12	15
Rejects	3	0

" Do you think the use of these expressions could keep a person from getting some types of jobs? "

32. Judgments as to Vocational Disadvantages, in Percentages

REPLIES	*Group S*	*Group D*
Yes	92	98
No	6	2
Rejects	2	0

" Do you think that some expressions common to a group may sound amusing and even laughable to some people of another group? "

33. Judgments as to Object of Ridicule, in Percentages

REPLIES	*Group S*	*Group D*
Yes	92	98
No	5	2
Rejects	3	0

" Do you agree that the dignity or standing of a racial or national group [7] is not helped by those whose speech may cause others to laugh at them? "

34. Judgments as to Dignity or Standing, in Percentages

REPLIES	*Group S*	*Group D*
Yes	70	89
No	23	10
Rejects	7	1

" If certain expressions may give the wrong idea about a person's ' learning ' and may cause some people to be laughed

[7] There may be some people who feel that some of the above questions may seem ambiguous, " loaded," and even cruel. My intention is not to hurt but to help. The ambiguity is the result of trying to word them so that all " yes " answers might be expected from the majority. They are " loaded " because this questionnaire was designed as a teaching instrument as well as a fact-finding one. They may be cruel because there are better ways of speeding progress than this type of shock treatment, which might bring on a guilt complex in some very sensitive students.

at, do you think it would help people to get along better together if they made more of an effort to overcome such expressions?"

35. Judgments as to Overcoming Disadvantages, in Percentages

REPLIES	*Group S*	*Group D*
Yes	92	94
No	5	6
Rejects	3	0

"Most people speak somewhat differently when speaking to family and friends from the way they speak in the classroom or to adults or strangers. Do you?"

36. Judgments as to Students' Levels of Speech, in Percentages

REPLIES	*Group S*	*Group D*
Yes	66	64
No	31	34
Rejects	3	2

37. Students' Evaluation of the Grammatical Correctness of Their Speech, in Percentages

SELF-EVALUATION	*Group S*	*Group D*
I always use good speech that is free from grammatical errors.	10	3
I use some slang expressions, but no grammatical errors.	28	31
I may use some grammatical errors and slang expressions.	50	60
I probably use many grammatical errors and slang expressions.	9	4
I use many of the expressions listed in this questionnaire.	3	2

A number of questions were designed to ascertain the students' evaluation of their own speech. They were asked: "How free from grammatical errors is your own speech to family and friends?" Table 37 shows their answers in percentages of each total group.

"If there is a wide grammatical difference between the speech you know how to use and the speech you do use when talking to your family and friends, can you give any reason why this should be?" The answers are arranged in Table 38 according to order of choice with percentages given for each group.

38. Students' Reasons for Using Non-Standard Grammatical Forms, in Percentages

REASONS	*Group S*	*Group D*
They'd think I was putting on airs.	28	8
They wouldn't understand me.	14	5
They'd think I was better than they.	10	3
They'd think I didn't belong to the group.	5	6
I have some other reason.	25	23
Rejects.	18	55

Some other reasons written in as requested include:

Just to be funny or to kid around.
When I talk to my family and friends, I talk like them.
I don't think about what I'm saying.
Because I have always used it.
I think everyone uses different speech at home.
I just don't try to impress anyone at home.
Speaking more freely at home.
I try to speak the way my family and friends do.
Not as important at home to speak correctly.
My parents would think I was crazy!
Because it's a symbol of teenagers.
No one notices.
Relaxed feeling and letting myself go. I'm more careful at school.

I don't think enough before speaking.
It is just a habit.
I believe that slang is sometimes used for emphasis, and grammatical errors just "slip out."
Because I am not used to it.
Just carelessness.
I read more than they.
Not on guard.

To the question: "Have you ever felt a need or a desire to use better grammar?" the answers, in percentages, of each group are given in Table 39.

39. Felt Need or Desire for Better Grammar, in Percentages

REPLIES	*Group S*	*Group D*
Yes	89	78
No	5	19
Rejects	6	3

Those who replied, "Yes," were asked at approximately what age they began to feel such a need or desire. Age 14 received the most checks for the S Group, and 16, for the D Group. Table 40 tabulates the answers.

40. Age at Which Student Felt Need or Desire for Better Grammar, in Percentages

AGE	*Group S*	*Group D*
6	2	0
8	3	2
10	5	4
12	20	9
14	34	23
16	24	35
18	2	5
20	0	0
Rejects	10	22

Table 41 shows the ten factors, out of twenty-two possible motivational or purpose-directing factors (questionnaire numbers 72 and 73), that, ranked highest in order of importance (1-10), received the greatest number of checks. There is a significant drop in the number of choices after the first five motivations.

41. Ten Motivational Factors Out of 22 Ranked Highest in Order of Importance

MOTIVATION	*Groups S & D*	*Group S*	*Group D*
A book or books	1	2	1
A friend of the opposite sex	2	1	3
A job situation	3	5	2
A teacher	3	3	5
An embarrassing moment	4	4	4
A parent	6	6	7
A new interest	7	7	8
Some other speech-making situation	8	9	8
A church situation	9	8	9
An adult you admired	10	10	6

Twenty-two items were listed after the question (numbers 74 and 75): "From your own experience, which of the following methods do you think help the most to improve speech? You may mark as many as five." These are arranged in Table 42 according to the students' choices, in order of importance, based on their total checks.

42. Methods of Speech Improvement, Ranked by Students in Order of Importance

METHODS	*Groups S & D*	*Group S*	*Group D*
Corrections by parents or friends	1	2	3
Corrections by teachers	2	1	7
Explanations by teachers	3	3	2

	Groups S & D	*Group S*	*Group D*
Hearing correct forms spoken at home	4	8	1
Hearing correct forms spoken at school	5	5	4
Original compositions which you rewrite to correct your errors	6	4	5
Written exercises (corrected and discussed) in which you choose correct forms	7	6	6
Oral talks with class corrections of errors	8	7	9
Oral grammar drills in which you indicate whether a statement is correct or incorrect	9	9	10
Written exercises in which you write sentences using certain forms of grammar	10	10	17
Oral talks with corrections given by the teacher	11	11	11
Hearing correct forms spoken at church, theatre, club, or on the job	12	14	8
Explanations read from textbooks or workbooks	13	12	14
Oral talks with written correction by the class and teacher	14	13	15
Hearing correct forms spoken in movies or on radio and television	15	15	13
Class and individual attention to correcting a few errors at a time	16	16	18
Hearing correct forms spoken elsewhere	17	19	12
Class games for pointing out each other's errors	18	17	21
Oral grammar drills in which you choose correct forms	19	20	16
Oral repeating of correct forms	20	19	19
Writing errors on pocket cards to be carried until the errors are overcome	21	21	22
Some other method	22	22	20

When asked to list other expressions used by members of

their group (questionnaire number 76) students were cooperative. An interesting list resulted, of which I give a few classified examples:

1. DOUBLE NEGATIVES: *I ain't done nothin', I don't know no better,* and *Don't say nothin'.*

2. LACK OF AGREEMENT: *We's a goin', I means it,* and *Is you listenin'?*

3. TROUBLE WITH VERB *be*: *He never be's home, I be done,* and *How you be?*

4. OMISSION OF AUXILIARIES: *What you talkin' 'bout? You wrong,* and *Why you say that?*

5. SLANG: *Real cool man! For real? It makes me no difference!*

6. DISPLACED LOCALISMS: *Hush you' mouf! This here'n, I axed him.*

7. PRONUNCIATION: *Who's dat? Wif him, Dere is.*

The questionnaire also asked the students to list " other good ways of correcting language." Their answers, some of which are below, fell into two classifications:

SUGGESTIONS DIRECTED TO STUDENTS:

1. *Use little sentences and gradually build up to bigger ones.*
2. *Let teachers, parents, and other people correct you without thinking they consider themselves better than you.*
3. *Speak slowly and think before you speak.*
4. *Listen to other people who know good speech and learn from them.*
5. *Study a foreign language.*
6. *Listen to good radio and television speakers and imitate them.*
7. *Go into your bedroom and talk to yourself.*

SUGGESTIONS DIRECTED TO TEACHERS:

1. *We don't seem to understand the complex words used in distinguishing parts of speech.*
2. *Have special instructors help those who have trouble with grammar.*

3. *Teachers are afraid to correct students in front of the class. Why?*
4. *Have more class discussion.*
5. *Show the individual the necessity for a fluent command of his language. Teach babies the importance of good speech.*
6. *Use recordings and listening to conversations between students.*

One student wrote, " Put two people together like letting them work together on a special project, and in a few days the person who has exceedingly poor speech will reform somewhat to the person with the good speech. Your environment is the best aid, I think."

Asked to name any books, plays, television programs, movies, or film strips they " think are especially good in helping people to get along better together," the students, again, were very cooperative. Because their answers were so varied, and often misplaced or misnamed, only a sampling of the titles is listed:

BOOKS (NON-FICTION):

The Bible
How to Win Friends and Influence People
How to Get Along With Other People
Improving Human Relations
Our World
Family Circle
Personal Adjustments in Marriage
Civic Leadership
Getting Along With Others
Understanding People
Your Family and You
The Power of Positive Thinking
Feelings are Facts

BOOKS (FICTION):

The Robe
A Man Called Peter

All-American
Going on Seventeen
Sea of Glory
Young Man About Town
Angel Unaware
The Greatest Story Ever Told
Playing Fair
The Stranger Beside Me
Seventeen Summers
Beneath This Tree
Perfect Gentlemen
Tiger of the Snows

PLAYS:

Our Town
Our Very Own
Teahouse of the August Moon
Good Morning, Parson

TELEVISION PROGRAMS:

Medic
Omnibus
Mama
Life is Worth Living
Ozzie and Harriet
I Love Lucy
Stu Erwin
Our Miss Brooks
Wide, Wide World
Disneyland
Fireside Theatre

MOVIES OR FILM STRIPS:

Blackboard Jungle
A Man Called Peter
The Egyptian
Waterfront
The High Wall
Prejudice
The House I Live In

The Joe Louis Story
The Good Earth

The last section of the questionnaire asked students to name any books (other than school books), plays, television programs, movies or film strips they " think are especially good in helping people to speak better." A sampling of the answers follows:

BOOKS:

Using Speech Correctly
Watch Your English
Are You Word Wise?
The Book of Etiquette
How to Speak Correct English
Knowing Your Grammar
How Do You Rate?
Emily Post
Ways to Improve Your Speech

PLAYS:

Pygmalion
Julius Caesar

TELEVISION PROGRAMS:

Hallmark Hall of Fame
Robert Montgomery Presents
$64,000 Question
You Bet Your Life
World Adventure Series
Also, news commentations, speeches, panel discussions, commercials, and educational programs.

MOVIES OR FILM STRIPS:

Johnny Belinda
Trial
Three Coins in a Fountain
News Magazine of the Screen
To Hell and Back
Moby Dick
Educational film strips

5 *Summary of the Findings*

The returns of the questionnaire show that patterns of non-standard speech are heard and used by those students whose families are mainly from the South. The patterns have their origins in archaic English and are now foreign to the general speech patterns of the Detroit area, but they have been, and are continuing to be, retained because of the social isolation of the users. Causes for the existing language situation go beyond the scope of this study and have been merely indicated.

The findings are based on uneven groups numerically, through circumstances beyond my control. Had the data from the other school of predominantly white population (Denby) been included, differences probably would have been more pronounced. Instead, the S group, which represents the Southern patterns, has received the advantage of the lack. The sampling is large, and results are given in percentages of each group so that figures are comparable. Since these returns are only from eleventh and twelfth grade students (71 per cent twelfth grade), they indicate a serious problem for the whole high school.

Based on the average number of checks for each expression, given in percentages, students in Group S checked the non-standard expressions as heard and used approximately four times as frequently as did the students in Group D, who represent the more general speech patterns of the Detroit area. (Table 1)

From one-half to four-fifths of the students in Group S checked as "heard" thirty non-standard expressions as compared to only two checked by half or more of the students in Group D. One-third to one-half of those in Group S checked as "heard" thirty-nine expressions as compared to three checked from the same range in Group D. (Table 2) Students in Group S are, therefore, at a disadvantage when competing with students of Group D in any endeavor in which judgment is based upon one of the most important tools in life–speech.

Fifty-six of the 102 expressions in the questionnaire are listed as ones showing the greatest differential in the speech patterns. They are gained by subtracting the percentages of Group D who checked each expression from the percentages in Group S who checked each. Seven of the expressions, shown by this study as characteristic of the S Group speech patterns, are as follows: *Yes, it do!, That's mines, It's fifty cent, Yes, you is!, I works hard, She say,* and *He have a–*. They are heard by 50-59 per cent more students in Group S than in Group D and are used by 22-38 per cent more in Group S than in Group D. The differential (by subtraction), shown in Table 3, for *Yes, it do!* in the "heard" column is 59 per cent, with a 30 per cent differential in the "graduates use" column, and 38 per cent in the "you use" column. For *That's mines,* the differential figures are 56 per cent, 27 per cent, and 29 per cent. In some cases, more students admitted using the expressions themselves more often than they heard high-school graduates use them.

Since students in Group S are shown to be in great need of speech correction, a knowledge of their backgrounds is important so that there can be greater understanding of how their need can be met.

In Group S, 48 per cent of the fathers are employed in semi-skilled work, and 41 per cent of the mothers are housewives with husbands employed. In Group D, 48 per cent of the fathers are employed in skilled jobs, while 53 per cent of the mothers are housewives with husbands employed. (Tables 4 and 5)

The relation between the expressions used and the father's occupational status shows that as the economic level is lowered, the expressions are more frequently used. Also, in regard to the often-heard expressions, the higher the occupational status of the mother, the less frequently are the expressions heard, but the relation between the father's occupational status and the expressions heard shows little change. (Tables 6, 7, 8) The latter indicates either that the relationship between the father and the child is not so close as that between the mother and the child or that the amount of hearing of the expressions goes on regardless of the occupational status of the father, because these students are seldom completely removed from the group as a whole. One may also conclude that those with higher economic status are perhaps more aware of hearing the expressions or are more free to admit hearing them.

Forty-five per cent of the students in Group S were born in Detroit, and 63 per cent started school here. (Table 9) Although educated in Detroit schools, an average of 27 per cent of the S Group admitted *using* thirty non-standard expressions, and an average of 31 per cent checked having *heard high-school graduates use* them. For these same expressions, in Group D an average of 7 per cent admitted *using* them and 11.5 per cent had *heard high-school graduates use* them, although 82 per cent of their group started school in Detroit. (Tables 2 and 9) These figures indicate that any change in teaching techniques which gives promise of showing better results should be welcomed.

Twenty-five per cent of the S Group were born in Alabama, Georgia, or Mississippi, Alabama accounting for 13 per cent. The rest were scattered, with only 6 per cent in locations other than the South. (Table 9)

Table 10 shows that the expression *Yes, it do!* is used by 50 per cent of those born in Georgia, and 42.6 per cent of those born in Alabama. The greatest users of *That's mines* are the 48.5 per cent of those born in Mississippi, the 39.5 per cent born in Georgia, and the 32.5 per cent of those born in Alabama. Still, 28.5 per cent of those born in Detroit use *That's mines,* and 37.9 per cent of those born in Detroit use *Yes, it do!*

The percentage of students reared by their mothers for Group S is 85 per cent and for Group D, 93.8 per cent. (Table 11) Those reared by the mother both heard and used the expressions more frequently than those reared by some other person. Perhaps in situations where the child is reared by another, a purpose has been to better the child, in which case this study would indicate positive results, although the average percentage of differential is only 17.2 per cent for expressions heard and 6.8 per cent for those used. (Table 12)

Twenty-one per cent more students in Group D than in Group S lived with both parents during the first five years, when the speech pattern was being formed. Some, but very little, variation occurred when the expressions often heard were related to those with whom the students lived, a factor indicating security. *Yes, it do!* was heard by 7 per cent fewer students who lived with both parents during their first five years than by those who lived with some other person. *That's mines,* was heard 9 per cent more frequently by those who lived with the mother or father alone than by those who lived with both parents. (Tables 13 and 14)

The educational level of the fathers is similar for both groups, in that Grade 9 or 10 is average for both groups, but there are more fathers with education above Grade 10 in the S group than in the D Group. The average level of education for mothers in the S group is Grade 9 or 10 while for the D Group it is Grade 11 or 12. In general, in both groups the mothers are more highly educated than the fathers. (Tables 15 and 17)

As the education of the mothers advances, fewer of the non-standard expressions are indicated as used and heard. In a few cases, expressions are used approximately 20 per cent less by those with more highly educated mothers. A surprising 32 per cent increase in the heard column occurs for the expression, *He graduate last June.* Perhaps more college-educated mothers have occasion to use this expression, but they probably still drop the *ed.*

Yes, it do! in Table 16 shows approximately an 8 per cent difference in the heard column and a little more than a 16 per cent difference in the amount of use indicated as the education of the mother advances. In Table 18, when this expression is related to the education of the father, the difference is approximately 7 per cent for heard and 29 per cent for used. *That's mines* shows a 21 per cent drop in hearing and a 9 per cent drop in the amount of use of the expression when those whose mothers have a fourth grade or less education are compared to those with some college education. The difference in the education of the fathers for *That's mines* is approximately 19 per cent for heard and 17 per cent for used. As should be expected, these tables show that speech does improve with education.

As indicated in Table 19, less than half of the students in both groups take a daily newspaper, but 30 per cent in the S Group take two periodicals and 32 per cent in the D Group take three. *Yes, it do!* was heard by 70 per cent of those who took only one periodical and by 70.7 per cent of those who took three or more, but was used 2.1 per cent less by those with three or more periodicals in the home. For *That's mines,* the drop in heard was less than 1 per cent, but in used was 4.6 per cent. Each of the other expressions, however, was used consistently less frequently by those who have more reading matter in the home. There is a positive relationship between the number of newspapers and periodicals brought regularly into the home and better speech usage. (Table 20)

Table 21 shows that 45 per cent of the students in the S Group have less than twenty books in the home while 48 per cent of the students in Group D have fifty or more. As an exception to the general picture of Table 22, *Yes, it do!* is heard 5 per cent more frequently by those with fifty or more books in the home than by those with less than ten, but there was a 12 per cent drop in use by those with more books. It is very probable that better educated students are more aware of hearing such an expression. *That's mines* showed a drop in heard of 8 per cent, and a drop in use of 10 per cent because of more books in the home library.

There is a relationship between the number of books in the home and the quality of speech. Those with more books used these expressions almost consistently less frequently. Reading background has definite bearing on speech usage.

Students in the S Group, according to Table 23, maintain more frequent church attendance, since 55 per cent attend usually once a week as compared to 52 per cent in Group D. Attending more often than once a week are 23 per cent of Group S and only 15 per cent of Group D. Nine out of twelve expressions, however, as shown in Table 24, were checked as often heard by a greater percentage of those who attended religious services than by those who practically never attended. It is highly possible that the pattern heard in religious services by many students of Group S may not help to improve their speech. Because there may be a greater number of smaller churches attended by the S Group than by the D Group, the educational backgrounds of the ministers may not be comparable. To ascertain the comparative quality of the speech patterns heard in religious services attended by the two groups would be a study in itself.

Attitude toward speech, and possibly toward the questionnaire, is indicated by answers to a series of questions which precede and follow the expressions. For an excellent attitude, *yes* answers were expected. That the attitude was very good is shown by the preponderance of *yes* answers in Tables 25 through 35. The highest percentage of *no* answers was 15 per cent for the D Group and 23 per cent for the S Group. Since many of the questions involved emotion, especially for those of the S Group, and one or two were ambiguously worded so as to evoke a *yes* answer, the attitude, in general, may be said to have been very cooperative and satisfactory.

The question indicated by Table 36 led into the self-evaluation of the testee's own speech. Sixty-six per cent in the S Group and 64 per cent in the D Group indicated that they spoke somewhat differently when speaking to family and friends from the way they speak in the classroom or to adults or strangers. At least half in both groups admitted the use of some grammatical errors and colloquial or slang expressions. There were more in Group S who thought they always used " good " speech than there were in Group D, but also more of the former who admitted using " poor " speech. (Table 37)

Table 38 shows that 28 per cent of the S Group indicated that they thought they would be *putting on airs* as the reason why there might be a wide grammatical difference between the speech they know how to use and the speech they do use when talking to their family and friends, and 25 per cent checked that they had *some other reason*. In the D Group 8 per cent checked the former reason, and 23 per cent the latter. There were 55 per cent rejects in the D Group to this question, but only 18 per cent in the S Group. Some of the other reasons written in and tabulated for both groups included such reasons as " carelessness," " habit," " relaxation," and the fact that " no one noticed."

The greatest percentage of students in Group S indicated that they felt a need or a desire for better grammar at the age of fourteen, and those in the D Group at the age of sixteen. (Table 40)

For motivational factors for improvement, both groups taken together ranked " a book or books " in first place, " a friend of the opposite sex " second, " a job situation " and " a teacher " third, and " an embarrassing moment " fourth. Taken separately, the S Group placed " a friend of the opposite sex " first and " a book or books " second, while the D Group placed " a book or books " first and " a job situation " second. The D Group placed " a teacher " in fifth place while the S Group placed " a teacher " third. (Table 41)

Both groups taken together ranked their preference in teaching techniques in the following order for the first five: " Corrections by parents or friends," " corrections by teachers," " explanations by teachers," " hearing correct forms spoken at home," and " hearing correct forms spoken at school." The S

Group, however, placed " corrections by teachers " in first place and " hearing correct forms spoken at home " in eighth place, while the D Group placed " hearing correct forms spoken at home " first and " corrections by teachers " in seventh place.

Out of twenty-two possible ratings, both groups together ranked " original compositions which you rewrite to correct your errors," " written exercises (corrected and discussed) in which you choose correct forms," and " oral talks with class corrections of errors " sixth, seventh, and eighth. (Table 42)

Additional non-standard expressions written in by the students included such groups as double negatives, lack of agreement, misuse of the verb *be*, omission of auxiliaries, slang, localisms and faulty enunciation. The students offered many good suggestions for correcting language directed to themselves and to teachers.

The lists of supplementary material the students submitted are interesting because they indicate the popularity of certain selections, but they are by no means comprehensive. For an excellent list of all types of materials pertaining to Negroes, I suggest *We Build Together*, by Charlemae Rollins. Other sources of material for helping people get along better together are cited in the footnote.[1] *The Check List of Books and Equipment in Speech from the 1956 Annual Directory* of the Speech Association of America is a comprehensive bibliography of speech materials.

The questionnaire revealed speech faults and some of the reasons why they persist. To satisfy the needs of our students we must find ways to correct their existing usage problems. Detection precedes correction, and where others note a similarity of conditions, the conclusions may have implication.

[1] The National Association for Mental Health, Inc., 1790 Broadway, New York 19; The National Conference of Christians and Jews, 381 Fourth Avenue, New York 16; Michigan Department of Mental Health, Lansing 16, Michigan; Detroit Round Table of the National Conference of Christians and Jews, 81 East Kirby, Detroit 2; Jewish Community Council of Metropolitan Detroit, Fred M. Butzel Memorial Building, 163 Madison Avenue, Dertoit 26; Michigan Regional Office of the Anti-Defamation League of B'Nai B'rith, 140 Cadillac Square, Detroit 26.

PART TWO

Possible Ways to Meet the Problem

6 *Changing Language Patterns*

There is a real English language problem in many areas. A great number of high school students have speech patterns containing historical, regional, foreign language, or other types of speech peculiarities that are not acceptable according to the general standards of a particular area. These students are at a disadvantage socially and vocationally. When they are competing for certain types of jobs for which they might otherwise be well qualified, reverting under stress to their non-standard patterns of speech could give a false impression of ignorance.

The problem is a general one, that of finding ways to help a student change his language patterns, whether his situation involves a change from the patterns of a Polish-speaking background, a Puerto Rican background, or that of any displaced person. It is purely a cultural matter having no biological basis.

The speech of many of our students, described in lay terms for high-school teaching use, may be characterized as including, as shown in Part I, a misuse of *be* in such expressions as, " He *be's* absent "; a misuse or omission of " s " in expressions like " It's mine*s*," and " ten cent–"; and all types of verb trouble, from omission of the auxiliary to lack of agreement with the subject and confusion of tense forms.

Whether or not these same language troubles are problems of other groups as well is of little significance compared to the fact that we do have a language problem and that our students need help.

While it is conceivable that many expressions, taken singly, could be used by some cultured speakers in some communities and in some situations, certain expressions are not acceptable as good informal speech in the Detroit area. They may be accepted as good meaning-carrying words in a smaller group within the area, but the problem exists because many of the users of this speech have come here hoping to take an active part, as the non-users have, in the social and economic life of the larger community. Students depend on the schools to effect the change in language usage, although their own tendency is so frequently to revert to their original language once they step out of school.

There are those who believe that the best procedure for our particular speech problem is a *laissez-faire* attitude. Those who favor this philosophy contend that since our problem is largely a socio-economic one, Father Time will take care of it. They believe we should continue with the type of language teaching we have been using with perhaps a little greater emphasis on upholding examples of correct forms. They dislike a direct approach to the problem, because they may not yet have grasped the full meaning of the concept of education for all American youth, or simply because of the fact that language is a personal thing about which we are all sensitive, and they fear offending.

Any attempt at a direct approach must be made with full consideration of the reasons for the *laissez-faire* attitude. However, that we should attempt to find effective ways to meet the needs of our students is in line with all good educational philosophy. " Start where they are with what they need," is a familiar pedagogical admonition.

Among the major reasons for this language difficulty is the lack of adequate reading background. More remedial reading classes are in order, and more emphasis must be placed on getting the child to read by introducing him to books on his own level of interest and ability. Lacking adequate sources for imitation during his formative years, he must now be given words and patterns of correct usage through the printed page. He must also be taught to sense the difference in style between written English and standard spoken English.

Something which we have already tried with a fair measure of success, and which we should encourage still further, is the use of such carefully selected paperback books as those put out by the Teen Age Book Club. We have done this by purchasing a quantity of the books in advance, requiring each student to buy one which he may select as he would select a library book. Then we build up a trading library, and the students trade among themselves. In this way the student may read any number of books for the cost of one. Librarians agree that getting the students to read by starting them on the popular paperbacks helps the library habit rather than encroaches on it. We stamp all school-purchased books with the school stamp as proof that they are sanctioned reading.

Reading kits such as those put out by Science Research Associates, whereby the student starts at his own level and competes with himself and the clock for developmental reading improvement, hold much promise.

Of course, good language teaching must begin early, just as good reading habits should be acquired early. Like the sentence used to correct other habits, " We don't do that in nursery school," perhaps more of " We don't say it that way. We say —— " would be in order. Certainly courtesy and confidence in speaking are more important than correctness, but teachers should give thought to the statement that " Practice doesn't make perfect; it makes permanent." Allowing continuous practice in unacceptable forms establishes them more firmly. While alertness is focused on making other adjustments to the new community, language adjustments must also be made. This can be brought about without harming the child psychologically.

As for teen-agers, setting up a few more desirable standards, in general, will help rather than hurt most of today's young people. Most of them want to be corrected because they want to be right, and if the rapport is good, corrections can be made without undue embarrassment.

The movement for giving foreign language training on the elementary level should have a good effect as an indirect solution. One may ask, " Why try to teach students a foreign language when they can't speak English? " Although the foreign language teachers will say that their purpose is purely cultural, especially since they now use the conversation approach, there are valuable by-products for speech training. Students will become aware of language as a tool at a time when language can fascinate them. Any type of phonetic practice will develop both oral and aural consciousness, the lack of which seems to be one key to our problem.

For a more direct approach to a solution, we must first bring about awareness of the need for a change, and this can best be done by letting the student hear himself as others hear him, through the use of recording and listening devices. The establishment of an English language laboratory, or studio class, for language practice in the high school seems to offer the most promise as a way to change poor language patterns to better ones. The second semester of high-school English seems the logical place for it as a class, and as facilities are developed, the laboratory could then be open to other students on an extra-credit, or purely voluntary, basis. Dividing a class into groups and providing tape recorders whereby the students can get practice in speaking and listening for their own improvement should bring results. Other audio-visual aids should be used to fullest advantage. Most schools have some of this equipment, but little provision has been made for its use. Actually turning a regular semester's composition course into a language laboratory would make this use possible. Self-direction and self-improvement should result, with the tape recorder doing a big part of the teaching. Various types of speech and composition activities could be carried on using group teaching techniques.

A Teen Talkers Club, a Teen Tapers Club, or a combination, should be organized.[1] These are modern versions of a

[1] In 1955-56 Teen Tapers clubs were sponsored by Tape Recording, Severna Park, Maryland, on a national scale. There were no national dues nor obligations, but national club news was carried in the Teen Tapers column of *Tape Recording Magazine,* which is no longer published by that title. *Hi-Fi Tape Recording* is now published monthly by the company.

Good English or a Better Speech Club but bear a more popular name to give them higher status. Membership in the Teen Talkers Club could be a pre-requisite to membership in the Teen Tapers Club and could serve as a training ground for the latter, or the Teen Tapers could be the governing body of a larger, honorary group. The success of both would depend upon making them so popular that many would strive for speech improvement to be eligible.

Another attack on the problem to effect awareness of the need might be in the form of a school-wide Better Speech Campaign, possibly sponsored by the Student Council and the Teen Tapers or Teen Talkers Club. This could start off with a tag day when all students would wear tags on which they wrote the faulty usages they heard. The campaign should run for possibly six weeks, taking ten minutes each day of the first week and continuing thereafter with appropriate assembly programs once a week. The campaign material, in duplicate copies, should be presented in each classroom.

In the teaching of language, certain units of work should be carefully developed. The historical approach to language should be explored so that students will see that the patterns of speech many of them are using are old-fashioned. It must be stressed that there is nothing wrong with these patterns, but they are like an old suit of clothes which one should not discard completely, because it may have its uses, but it would be out of place if worn in most social situations.

There should be a good unit on the new approach to basic grammar so that students can understand the grammar of position, the structure words, and the changing word forms.

As teachers, we must avoid wasting time on trivialities and on the controversial usages that have become acceptable. We should not try to adhere to written standards when our students have not yet acquired an acceptable standard for informal speech. We must be realistic. Furthermore, we must avoid doing much of the talking. It is the students who need the practice.

Drill games must be prepared for using the word forms that require changes in endings and within the words, but the drills must involve thought to be effective. Patterns that are acceptable as good speech must be set up for oral practice exercises, and techniques for vocabulary development must be pointed out.

Speech improvement must be self-improvement. We cannot change the student's patterns for him, but we can bring about awareness of a need for a change, aid him in finding ways to make the change, and encourage his efforts at self-improvement.

7 *The English Language Laboratory*

There seem to be at present no scientific data to prove that the use of tape recorders or phonograph records will bring about speech improvement. The act alone of hearing one's speech as others hear it indicates only that the hearer has heard. This act, which is often a surprising experience to the most confident of speakers, could, conceivably, have harmful results to a very reticent person if no therapy accompanies the hearing experience. Much depends upon the attitude and purpose of the listener, upon the interpretation of what he hears, and upon his efforts at self-improvement as a result of what he hears. Lacking scientific data, we are not in a position to suggest that the constructive use of tape recorders in a laboratory situation as described below will in any sense be a cure-all. It is, however, one avenue which should be explored.

For schools where students need help in changing language patterns, an English language laboratory offers interesting possibilities. It is designed to replace a regular composition course or to be used as a unit in a full-year English course. Since this study began, it has been tried at the Detroit Northeastern and Central high schools with encouraging results. First offered at Northeastern in the ninth grade, it is now being used with greater success at Central in the tenth grade. Because of the large class size and the inadequate physical arrangement in the schools, the older students, with greater seriousness of purpose, more easily adjust to the laboratory technique. At either level, the laboratory encourages good speech habits which should set the patterns for oral and written expression throughout life. Experiments to test its effectiveness are now in progress.

The laboratory initiated at Central High School at the 10A level was designed to function, for at least three of the five days a week, on a three-group plan with one group using ear phones for listening and repeating exercises *via* tape recorders, one group using the Science Research Associates Reading Kit, and one group working in a composition circle getting on-the-spot correction and help with writing. All were specially selected students who needed remedial work in some phase, or all phases, of English. Besides the SRA Reading Kit and listening tapes, which I prepared using exercises suggested in Chapter XII, we used mimeographed copies of Chapter XI, the *Practical English Magazine,* published by *Scholastic Magazines,* and my *The 3 Book, Communication Skills,* a handbook which reduces English essentials to a minimum. For a more detailed coverage of English usage, we plan to add to the materials the *Plain English Handbook* by J. Martyn and Anna Kathleen Walsh. As the remedial work progresses, we hope also to separate those primarily needing reading help into separate classes so that the English language laboratory can concentrate on helping those students who need to understand the structure of our language and need practice in using its standard forms.

The philosophy behind the laboratory is that, given the chance to hear himself as others hear him, the student may become his own best critic. He should be given the opportunity to hear and practice good speech forms until he feels comfortable in using them. The role of the teacher is to guide, to encourage, and to praise all attempts at self-improvement.

A large room with sixteen or more cubicles, each equipped with recording and listening mechanism, as in the foreign language laboratory in the new seven-million-dollar Ann Arbor (Michigan) High School or that at Georgetown University's Institute of Language and Linguistics, would be the ideal setting. But any large room partitioned off, or with smaller adjoining rooms for group work, would be adequate. If necessary, the auditorium, the stage, and dressing rooms would serve the purpose, providing there are trained student assistants for supervision. As many tape recorders as there are rooms or cubicles would be desirable. For each recorder where group work is to be carried on there should be an aggregate board equipped with phono-jack openings for plugging in earphones. This would allow several students to sit around a recorder listening to practice exercises seemingly directed to each personally through the earphones. Since each student repeats the exercises just loudly enough to hear himself say them, and only those with earphones can hear the taped messages, it is possible for this activity to be going on in a corner of a large classroom while the rest of the class is engaged in other work. Also desired for a complete English language laboratory would be a good supply of tape and as much audio-visual equipment, such as television, a record player and maker, a Language Master, as can be assembled.

Obviously, the smaller the group, the more individual the attention that can be given. The maximum should be twenty-five. Instead of a textbook, in areas where students buy their own, a fee could be charged to provide each student with a handbook, tape, and mimeographed materials. Library books, records, tapes, newspapers, and magazines could be used as well as sets of books and reading kits owned by the English Department.

Other than the pattern practice exercises, speech activity, in general, should follow this order: read, speak, listen, write. Some formal speeches should be written first, but the major emphasis should be on setting good informal speech patterns for every-day use, and activity should proceed with this end in view. Speech games of the many types developed by Marjorie Wescott Barrows should be used for developing better usage. These games, which younger students enjoy playing occasionally in class and older students enjoy knowing about for outside use, require students to think as they repeat better forms and hear them repeated by others.[1]

[1] Marjorie Wescott Barrows, *Good English Through Practice* (New York: Henry Holt and Co., Inc., 1956).

To initiate the language laboratory procedure, I suggest that the class first meet in one large group for introductions and orientation. With the students doing most of the talking, the teacher should discuss aims, procedures, conduct and levels of language and their uses as communication. He should emphasize that courtesy and fluency of speech are of more importance than correctness and that it is just as conspicuously unfashionable to be too precise in some situations as to be too slovenly; that maturing thought requires maturing speech; and that attention will be focused on developing good informal language usage.

He should discuss equipment, respect for it, and fairness in sharing it and decide which students should use tape first and which should give prepared talks first in case there are not enough recorders for each group.

He should discuss leadership and cooperation and choose leaders by the volunteer method, or by election or appointment. Groups may form around the leaders according to the students' choices except for suggestions by the teacher where necessary. Later, the groups may be reorganized according to interests or needs.

He should decide on a roll call system and on signals for general assembly; distribute the suggested activity lists; have groups meet to plan their discussion topics for getting started on outside reading and choices for speech assignments, in situations that permit the students to make choices. Groups should then report their plans to the general assembly, and group work is ready to begin.

Except for the repetition of taped drill lessons, or for other special projects, the work could follow this weekly plan:

MONDAY: *(Whole Class) General planning session and discussion of aims based on written criticisms and other written assignments.*

TUESDAY:
WEDNESDAY: *(Tape Recorder Groups) The following suggested activities should be taped in class and played back.*

THURSDAY:

1. *Impromptu reading followed by briefly expressing the thought in one's own words.*
2. *Impromptu speaking using the "Inquiring Reporter technique," illustrated below.*
3. *Reading, previously practiced, of short paragraphs containing needed forms, good patterns, or even tongue twisters for developing oral and aural consciousness.*
4. *Speech games and drill lessons for pattern practice.*
5. *Extempore talks of various types.*
6. *Group discussions on various topics.*

FRIDAY: *(Whole Class) General meeting for taped program assembled outside of class by a student committee. Written "Listening Papers," described below, should be prepared and handed in.*

Plans should be adjusted to meet the needs of groups which show initiative in wanting to do worth-while activities that fit the general aim.

On days when there is a good televised speech program, assignments which require good listening should be given, followed by a student-conducted discussion, taped and played back.

As an enrichment program service to the rest of the school, the class might invite other classes to send one or two students to hear a program and give a report on it to their class upon return. A letter-writing activity could be involved.

After skilled student assistants have been trained, the language laboratory, when not in use by a class, could be open by appointment to individuals from all grades. Expensive and valuable training equipment should seldom be idle.

Directions for Listening Papers (as given to students): Place proper identification heading at the top of the page. Fold the paper down the center. Label the left side GOOD, and the right side IMPROVE. Under these headings, write the speaker's name across the head at the center and write brief comments in both columns under GOOD and IMPROVE. Include specific language peculiarities, if any, under IMPROVE.

Valuable natural repetition of certain needed usages may be maneuvered by the careful planning of oral assignments. For example, to correct " *This mean*——," a list of quotations or short passages to be interpreted gives each student the opportunity to repeat, " *This means*——." Sayings from *Poor Richard's Almanac* serve this purpose very well. The teacher should call attention to the *s* and the reason for using it; then see that each student does use it.

When teaching capitalization, the teacher should emphasize the use of the diphthong [aI] in *capitalized.* He should drill on such words as *buy, sigh, tie, my, kind, ride, guide.* Then as each student in turn reads a drill sentence from his homework, he should make sure that he says, " I capitalized —— " and explains why. He should not substitute [æ] for the diphthong in *capitalized,* and know why he should not.

Student-made speech booklets containing speech drills, outlines of talks, pictures depicting speaking situations, etc., when presented orally to the class, give opportunity to emphasize many good usages, such as: " On this page —— " (not " this *here* page ") ; " This picture —— " (not " *pitcher* ") ; " These people are talking about —— " (not " *peoples are* ") ; " I have —— " (not " I *got* ") ; " In mine —— " (not " In *mines* "). In addition to good language values, the knowledge of learning how to hold a book for a demonstration talk and gaining ease in speaking before an audience through adding action to words can be acquired.

SUGGESTIVE ACTIVITY LIST. Activities are to be selected to meet the needs of individuals and of groups.

1. An informal talk entitled " About Me "
   (A getting-acquainted device)
2. A personal experience
   (May be imaginary)

3. The meeting (club, PTA, union, etc.)
   (Order of business, presenting and talking for a motion, reading the minutes, a committee report)
4. An informal discussion
   (Topics of interest such as dating, getting along with parents, sharing in the home)
5. A panel discussion
   (Book talks included here)
6. A talk intended to entertain
   (Examples below)
7. A talk intended to inform
   (Practical situations including how to make or do something)
8. A talk intended to convince
   (Practical situations such as registering a complaint or asking for a raise in salary)

EXAMPLES OF TALKS TO ENTERTAIN

1. White lies are permissible
2. If I were a teacher
3. The best way to see the country
4. Life without speech
5. Our house in a tree
6. The psychology of knowing when to ask for things
7. Faces in a bus
8. Having all the money I wish
9. Things I'd like to invent
10. Lunch hour
11. The milkman's thoughts at work
12. The care of your dog
13. Raising a parakeet

POSSIBLE SPECIAL PROJECTS

1. The Teen Talkers and Teen Tapers clubs
2. A school-wide better speech campaign
3. A unit of purposeful grammar
4. A vocabulary unit
5. A courtesy unit
6. A declamation contest

7. Panel discussion with community leaders
   (On youth problems, vocational opportunities and requirements, community needs, etc.)
8. An assembly program

TYPES OF DISCUSSION GUIDE QUESTIONS TO INITIATE THE COURSE

1. Why should this class be called a language laboratory? What is the purpose of a laboratory? Would we prefer to call it a studio?
2. What is language, and how important is it?
3. Why should maturing minds need maturing language?
4. How much truth is there in the saying, "As you speak, so you are"?
5. How has our language developed? (Volunteers for outside reading and reports.)
6. Are there levels or acceptable variations of language?
7. What is the level of the language of the students in our school? (Let's find out. For an assignment, write out a page of actual speech that you hear. It may be several bits of conversation, but it should be actually what you and your classmates say to each other.)
8. What level of speech should be our aim? (Try writing examples of the same thought expressed on different levels.)
9. What other qualities of speech are even more important than correctness?
10. Can you name any well-known persons whose speech you admire sufficiently to imitate?
11. How could we proceed to get the most use from the advantages we have in the laboratory? What types of activities could we try?
12. How do you think an ideal working group should function and get along together?
13. How should we conduct ourselves in a laboratory containing this valuable equipment? (Would you like to draw up, outside of class, a few rules that you think would be helpful? We could discuss them and have a committee resolve them to as few as possible.)
14. Because each person has an equal opportunity to use the equipment, does that mean that each will use it to an

exactly equal extent? Why? How does this work in other situations?

15. Is it natural that some people are leaders and some are followers, according to their different interests, but that both are needed? Who are some of the people in the room who would make good group leaders? Good secretaries? Good hosts or hostesses?

IMPROMPTU SPEAKING TOPICS OF THE INQUIRING REPORTER TYPE. *The following are suggestive of the kinds of questions the reporter might pursue to get the speaker to express at least one complete thought.*

1. Where do you spend your summer vacations?
2. What is your favorite hobby?
3. What are your favorite sports?
4. What school have you enjoyed going to most?
5. What type of school work do you like most?
6. What season of the year do you like most?
7. What do you intend to do after high school graduation?
8. What kind of books do you like to read?
9. What do you do for recreation?
10. Which theatre do you like best to attend?
11. What is your favorite television program?
12. Who is your favorite disc jockey?
13. Which radio programs are your favorites?
14. What kind of music do you like best?
15. What is the most exciting thing that has ever happened to you?
16. What was your most embarrassing moment?
17. When were you most afraid?
18. How many members are there in your family?
19. What is the location of your home?
20. Where do you spend your leisure time?
21. Have you ever had an accident?
22. Have you ever been in or witnessed an automobile accident?
23. Have you ever been up in a plane?
24. In what city or town were you born?
25. Who is your favorite movie star?

26. Have you had any unusual experience?
27. Has anything unusual happened to any members of your family?
28. Which holiday is your favorite?
29. Where and how do you spend most holidays?
30. Are you superstitious?
31. What do you think about our school football team?
32. What make of car is your favorite?
33. What parks do you like best?
34. How often do you go to the public library?
35. What do you think of our school paper?
36. To what school clubs do you belong?
37. Do you like to swim?
38. Do you have a part-time job after school?
39. What is your ambition?
40. How many members of your family or close relatives have been in service?
41. What do you like best to eat?
42. What do you like best to wear?
43. How long does it take you to get to school?
44. What do you do to help at home?
45. How do you try to show appreciation to your parents?
46. How often do you go downtown?
47. What is the nicest present you have ever received?
48. If you suddenly had $20.00 to spend, what would you do with it?
49. If you could take a trip right now, where would you go?
50. What is the farthest distance you have ever been from here?

8 *The Teen Talkers and Teen Tapers*

To encourage good language usage and general self-improvement is the purpose of the Teen Talkers and Teen Tapers clubs. As already mentioned, these clubs should be conducted in such a way that all students will wish to be members, but many will have to strive for improvement in language first. Since fluency, courtesy, and confidence in speaking bring their own rewards, emphasis here is on careful speech, characterized by good structure and good enunciation. Careful speech does not mean overly precise speech. It should be fluent and courteous and indicate confidence, but it must also show, in general, freedom from the use of unacceptable forms, overworked expressions, and poor enunciation and pronunciation.

Eligibility should be limited to high-school students who have good speech habits that meet the generally accepted language standards for the region in which they live and who attempt to use good English both in and out of school.

Members must be recommended, solely upon the basis of speech proficiency, by the English teachers either with or without the assistance of a class committee. Once the club is organized, the list of recommended members should be passed upon by the governing board and the sponsors. Students should know at least two weeks in advance that such a selection will be made.

Membership is honorary and entitles the recipient to wear a pin, to vote for the board and to attend any functions planned by the board. Membership in the Teen Talkers is a pre-requisite to becoming a Teen Taper and may be extended as a pre-requisite to participation in other activities. If only one speech club is desired, as was the case at Northeastern because of the number of existing clubs and heavy teacher schedules, the Teen Tapers serve as the governing board for the Teen Talkers. When first organized, 10 per cent of the Teen Talkers were elected as Teen Tapers. Since there were 150 students recommended by English teachers and initiated as Teen Talkers, 15 were elected Tapers. Two semesters later, because of increased enrollment and lengthened school day, it was decided that all Teen Talkers who happened to have no class at a certain hour would automatically be Teen Tapers. It is necessary to have a regular meeting time for the governing board to plan interesting activities, and attendance at meetings is always a problem in this type of teaching situation.

The governing body, the board, should consist of from seven to fifteen elected (or appointed, if necessary) members, a faculty sponsor, and a faculty assistant. The board (Teen Tapers, at Northeastern) should elect its own president, vice-president (program chairman), secretary, and treasurer. The remaining board members may serve as committee chairmen as the need arises.

The board should have regular business meetings and should plan suitable programs for the group-at-large. The group-at-large (Teen Talkers) may be contacted through the English classes, and occasionally brief class section meetings may be conducted during the English classes. They should meet for initiation or business at least two or three times a semester, and should be excused from classes to do so, if necessary. Since they are an honorary group, they should be invited at other times during the semester to attend school speech contests or special assembly programs.

Each member is presented with a pin which he should wear as a reminder that he is interested in self-improvement. Admission to special assemblies and field trips may be by pin plus any necessary fee. If a member loses his pin, he must write a letter explaining the circumstances to the board, and upon their approval, he may purchase a replacement. (At Northeastern

High School, since there was no money available for pins, printed campaign-button type pins were ordered, and each Teen Talker purchased his own.)

An initiate might be required to do such things as:

1. Refrain from chewing gum as a reminder that he is building good habits connected with his tongue, teeth, and lips.
2. Write a list of speech peculiarities that he especially wishes to avoid.
3. Write a list of good words which he wishes to add to his vocabulary.
4. Cut out examples of good English usage from newspapers and magazines and paste them on a sheet of colored paper with a heading cut from headline letters.
5. List overworked expressions and give for each five better ways to say the same idea.
6. Write a short composition or give a short speech on one of the following topics:
   a. What is communication?
   b. Why is good language important to me?
   c. What is good speech?
   d. What is meant by "levels of language"?
7. Find and explain a slogan pertaining to language.
8. Describe the speech used by the person whose speech you admire most.
9. Make a poster suitable for a Better Speech Campaign.

An appropriate pledge service might be prepared and repeated in unison at the pinning ceremony.

SUGGESTED PLEDGE

I pledge that I shall strive for self-improvement in every way possible. I shall respect the English language as this nation's means of communication and strive to use it effectively. I shall attempt to talk with a level of language that is clear, courteous, and concise. I shall strive for speech that is friendly and comfortable, neither bookish nor ungrammatical. I shall avoid using expressions which are overworked and those which are offensive to general standards of acceptance. Knowing that language re-

flects culture, and that culture is acquired through education, I shall give thought to our motto: " Speak well, live well."

Activities might include a welcoming tea; initiation of new members; a picnic; assembly programs with good speakers; field trips to lectures, speech contests, and plays; preparing the audio-visual order list for the English Department; and the planning and presentation of a Good English Drive or Better Speech Campaign.

9 *A Better Speech Campaign*

A school-wide Better Speech Campaign will be successful if the idea seems to come from the students themselves and if a nucleus of interested students can inspire the cooperation of the entire student body. It would be well to have it sponsored by two popular organizations such as the Teen Talkers Club and the Student Council with English classes serving as the working groups.

The recommended time is six weeks with the entire school devoting ten minutes a day at a certain time each day of the first week, and ten minutes on Mondays and Fridays for the next five weeks, with a voluntary follow-up thereafter. The campaign could be conducted in the English classes, but will be much more effective if the students get the feeling of sharing with everyone in the school an interest in improving language as a basic tool for all subjects. Homeroom, group, or record-taking time would be ideal with the period extended, if necessary.

Careful preparation is mandatory for a successful campaign. Mimeographed notices should be prepared to direct the campaign. These should be read and discussed in the classroom to call attention to the particular phases of speech improvement. Posters and PA system announcements should be prepared and plans made for a tag day. There should be a good assembly program once a week, which will require thorough preparation. The assembly should feature excellent speakers or appropriate films or plays.

I suggest the following learning experiences during preparation:

1. Letter writing to: the principal, the Teen Talkers Club, the Student Council, the Audio-Visual Department, the Art Department, the forensics coach, the drama coach, etc.
2. Invitations to speakers and play groups
3. Planning and discussion
4. Writing materials for improving speech
5. Making posters and tags

And these during the drive:

1. Cooperation
2. Inspiration
3. Awareness of the need for speech improvement
4. Awakening of a desire to improve
5. Acquisition of self-help techniques
6. Drill to establish new habits

Mimeographed notices to be distributed to each teacher could read as follows, or could be revised by a committee to fit the needs of a particular school:

Dear M____________.

The Better Speech Campaign, about which you have previously been informed, will start this coming Monday, and continue for six weeks. As you know, it is being sponsored by the Student Council and the Teen Talkers Club, and we hope you will be as enthusiastic about it as we are, for your enthusiasm is catching.

During the first week, the drive will take at least ten minutes of the group period each day, and as much additional time as you wish to give it. For the next five weeks, the school-wide campaign will take ten minutes or more on Mondays and Fridays, and, after that, we hope you will encourage good speech habits throughout the semester.

For each day of the drive, you will receive a mimeographed notice which we ask you to read to the class. It will tell what to do and serve as a guide to discussion.

Thank you for your cooperation.

Respectfully yours,

The Committee for the
Better Speech Campaign

The Better Speech Campaign Bulletin for Monday might read as follows: (The teacher reads to the class.)

Whether we admit it or not, most of us are here to acquire some of the tools and skills that will fit us to build a good life for ourselves and for those about us. Language is one of the most important of these tools. Good language is a key to success.

The Student Council and the Teen Talkers Club have chosen today as the starting date for a big all-school campaign to help all of us give thought to the levels of language we use and to strive for self-improvement through better self-expression. We solicit your cooperation.

Today is tag day. When this class is over and you step out into the hall, everyone will be wearing a tag, and everyone will be talking as usual. You will talk too, but you will also listen. If you hear an expression or a grammatical construction which you know is not generally accepted as good usage in this area, you will politely borrow the speaker's tag for a moment and write the expression on it.

Here are the rules:

1. *Be a good sport.*
2. *Ask and give the tag politely.*
3. *Don't argue. One little expression that someone* thought *he heard isn't that important.*
4. *Write clearly, but save space for others. The day is long, and the tag is short.*
5. *Practice saying, "May I—" or "Give me—" (not "Gimmie"), "Please" and "Thank you."*
6. *Don't worry if your tag is soon filled.*

Remember that good speech is clear, courteous, and correct. No one wants you to be bookish or to use formal, written standards for informal speech, but it is expected that the speech of high-school students should be free from non-standard expressions which are offensive to those who use good language.

You will hand in your tag tomorrow so that the types of language difficulties may be studied and your needs met. Your name will not be on your tag. It's cooperation that counts.

(*Not to be read to the class.*)

While the tags are being passed, the teacher asks the students to think of some of the non-standard expressions which may be written on the tags if heard. He discusses them with the class.

The list may include *I seen, you was, he have, pitcher* for *picture, mines, bein's, youse,* and *dey* for *they.*

He appoints two class secretaries to record the class campaign, and two people to help arrange a suitable bulletin board.

Tags, secretaries' reports, and other materials collected are to be turned in to the department head. Recognition will be given to the most cooperative homerooms.

The Bulletin for Tuesday: (The teacher reads the following, one sentence at a time, waiting for responses.)

Before you turn in your tags, you might like to take a minute or two to exchange and read them. . . . Pass them all to the front.

What expressions did you hear that were not mentioned yesterday? Tell what should have been said in each case. . . . Start a list in your notebook and for the rest of the week write down all of the faulty expressions you hear. After each expression, write one or two better ways to say it.

Is there a need for a speech campaign? . . . What can the campaign accomplish? . . . Who has to make the changes in speech? . . . What ideas do you have on ways that will help one to change his speech habits? . . . What could we do as a class that would be helpful?

Secretaries: Be sure to record all ways mentioned.

(*Take action on any good ideas.*)

Don't forget to keep your Listening Lists this week and hand them in Friday.

Add these words to your vocabulary if you don't already know them. Can you spell them correctly? (*Write them on the board so that they may be copied. Discuss meanings and pronunciation.*)

campaign	diligently
usage	peculiarities
fallacies	virtuoso
analogy	colloquialisms
attuned	vernacular

The Bulletin for Wednesday: (The teacher reads through and then discusses.)

Speech is a two-sided activity. It needs a listener as well as a speaker. How good a listener are you?

Listen carefully to this comparison of language to music and then discuss every thought of it. There may be some fallacies in the analogy:

Language is music played mainly by ear, but more beautiful if also played by note. Some people who play language completely by ear are never aware of their own discords. To correct discords and to become a master of music, one needs first to read notes and then to read them well. It is a rare person who can imitate the great music of the masters entirely by ear.

To learn by ear a language that is pleasing to others and that will serve us well, we must keep our ears attuned to the symbols which are accepted and understood by the majority. The best in music is that which is timeless because it has universal appeal.

We may entertain ourselves and our friends with the music of the moment just as all of us make use of the current slang phrases, but our basic pattern is best if it is harmonious to all. It will serve us best if it is that which is generally accepted as good usage or as good music.

If, as we grow up, we realize that the pattern of language which has surrounded us and which we have imitated or played by ear does not represent good music in the bigger orchestra of life in which we hope to play, then we must change or shift our style just as Nat King Cole shifted his style and tripled his earnings.

We must first attune our ears to the differences and analyze our pattern of language, or music, to detect the discordant notes. Then we must apply ourselves diligently to a study of the notes and rhythms which represent harmony to the vast majority of music lovers. We must not continue to play *A* flat if the music calls for *A* natural.

In language we may need to become as well acquainted with the traditional eight parts of speech as we would with the eight notes of the scale. But, of course, simply knowing the parts of speech or knowing the notes will not make either language or music melodious. We must know the various ways of putting the parts together so that we can express, through language, each shade of meaning that flashes into thought, just as, through music, all of the various moods of mankind may be expressed.

This shifting and perfecting of language pattern is not done easily or overnight. Nor does one suddenly become a piano virtuoso. As it takes continuous practice and many other factors to shift from being merely a chop-sticks player to being a good musician, so it takes practice and thought and desire and then more practice to shift into using the pattern that is universal, and to feel so much at home in the new pattern that we can truly "make music" with it.

ASSIGNMENT: Copy from books, or clip from newspapers or magazines, examples of correct usage. Choose usage patterns which we especially need to emphasize. If you use clippings, you, or a group of you, may want to paste them neatly on a sheet of colored paper. We will show and discuss them in class tomorrow.

HERE ARE SOME WASTEBASKET WORDS:

1. *shouldn't ought* (There are only two correct forms: *ought* and *ought not.*)
2. *disremember* (Say *forget.* It's shorter, too.)
3. *peoples* (You would be more correct if you never put an *s* on this word. The plural form is correct only when speaking of nations.)
4. *youse* (*You* is both singular and plural.)
5. *unlessen* (The word is *unless.*)
6. *irregardless* (the word is *regardless.*)
7. *onliest* (The word is *only.*)
8. *complected* (The word is *complexioned.*)
9. *fixing to* (This is an overworked and meaningless expression. Say what you mean.)
10. *wa'n't* (Say *wasn't* or *weren't.*)

The Bulletin for Thursday: (The teacher interrogates the class and discusses.)

How are you progressing with your own individual speech problems? Are you choosing one or two expressions to work on until corrected? Many people write these on little pocket cards which they carry as reminders until the cards can safely be thrown away. Then they write new ones with new corrections to be made.

Have you learned by now that good speech need not be stilted speech? Good speech is friendly, clear, and comfortable speech, but it is structurally sound and in fashion. Why be comfortable in a horse-drawn buggy when most high-school people feel more comfortable in an automobile?

There is nothing really wrong about these expressions you choose to discard, just as there is nothing wrong about a horse and buggy or your old pair of work pants. They serve you well in some situations. For some people who haven't had your opportunities to get ahead, these expressions serve very well as a means of communicating meaning. We won't laugh at those who use them or pity them. We'll understand but try even harder for individual self-improvement.

Pronounce these sentences carefully: (*Other schools may want to substitute other sentences meeting their needs.*)

1. It was du*r*ing the day.
2. The men h*e*lpe*d* me.
3. He'*s* *a*bsent.
4. He ha*s* a pi*ct*ure of a pitcher.
5. It cos*ts* ten cen*ts*.
6. The people are here, *aren't* they?
7. She will be grad*u*ated in Ja*nua*ry.
8. He *took* my *pencil*.
9. That dea*th* was *th*is mon*th*.
10. He'*s* the *only* chil*d* here.

You may want to copy them in your notebook for continued drill.

Share your good usage lists and clippings with the class now, and bring your Listening Lists tomorrow.

The Bulletin for Friday: (The teacher addresses the class.)

Today is the last day of our intensive Better Speech Campaign, but good speech must go on. During the next five weeks on Mondays and Fridays we will take up work on some of the particular kinds of usages which should be improved, but you must practice good speech habits every day of the week.

We shall now read, discuss, and hand in the Listening Lists you have been keeping all week. Then we shall hear reports from the Bulletin Board chairmen, and the secretaries will read their reports before handing them in. In this way we can summarize and evaluate our week's work.

The tabulation of non-standard usages recorded during the first week of Northeastern High School's Better Speech Campaign, following the above plan, showed some interesting results.

Out of a total of approximately 1,600 items listed by students and turned in to the Teen Talkers, there were at least 265 different faulty usages. Slovenly enunciation caused by lip-laziness accounted for 452 of the total items.

Gimme was objected to as used and recorded 113 times. Various uses of *ain't* were found objectionable. Uses of *ain't* included 349 substitutions of *ain't* for *am, is,* or *are not,* and 71 substitutions of *ain't* for *haven't.* There were 77 uses of *ain't* with a double negative. Two choice *ain't* expressions were *Ain't they did it?* and *I ain't ginny ya nothin'.* There were 28 other double negative usages including *He didn't told me nothing.*

One hundred and thirteen discourteous interjections such as *hey, yeh* or *yeah,* and *naw* were itemized. There were 87 non-standard expressions including *ya'all* (singular), *youse, unlessen, axe, fixin' to,* and *disremember.*

Faulty usages in tense of verbs occurred 83 times with *I done* and *I seen* rating highest. Expressions involving lack of agreement between subject and verb were recorded 56 times. Of these, *Is you goin'* scored highest with a count of 14.

Omission of the auxiliary verb accounted for 55 expressions, such as *She gone,* and *I been.* Four students confused *leave* with *let,* and three substituted *learn* for *teach.*

There were 56 examples of "misplaced" *s,* not counting those in non-standard verb agreement. *Mines* was recorded 17 times and *peoples,* 27.

Use of the objective case (*me, us, them*) for the subject was recorded 12 times, and there were 6 examples of double subjects.

Twenty-six good usages were recorded. Either the writers didn't know the difference, or they heard errors but wrote the correct forms.

As a result of the campaign, Northeastern High School students gained in speech consciousness and awareness of the need for speech improvement. This was evidenced by the apparent frequency with which they were overheard correcting each other. Further evidence of interest in the campaign was the fact that after the 55 posters made by Teen Talkers were taken down at the end of the first week, just as many more appeared as the spontaneous contribution from other students.

The memory of the speech campaign even in later years may remind faltering Falcons to " look up, and speak well! "

There is no way of measuring the number of students who may have been influenced by a message in a poster or a cartoon, such as the one shown below, which was published in the school newspaper.

10 *The Pendulum Swings in Language Teaching*

The subject of language teaching is one of great interest at present. English teachers have been accused of entertaining "fancy notions about the status of language," and it has been said that "we have treated our students as culpable transgressors against their language and nagged them out of all normal pleasure in it." Teachers of English are pictured as desk-bound purists insisting on written standards with little feeling for language as it is actually spoken. How true is this charge, and how far should such thinking go?

Just as conflict is an important ingredient that focuses attention in fiction, so it is a welcome element in the field of teaching English. Once discussed as "rules *versus* usage," and then as "structural *versus* Latin grammar," the controversy has many facets and has attracted much-needed attention.[1] Students who cannot trust the usage they hear may need a few simple rules to help them learn good language. Simple rules, however, may be inaccurate; yet clarifying the inaccuracies may require pages of explanation. Structural grammar is simpler and more accurate, but as yet there are few materials to aid the teacher in presenting it, and many who depend upon the prior knowledge of Latin grammar feel that it means added, rather than less, nomenclature.

Two extreme viewpoints on language and language teaching continue to prevail: that of the pre-scientific, traditional school, or Latin grammarian, and that of the modern scientific gram-

[1] Wallace L. Anderson, "Structural Linguistics: Some Implications and Applications," *The English Journal,* XLVI (1957), 410.

marian, or linguist. The modern view is ably presented in *American English in its Cultural Setting,* a new college textbook by Donald Lloyd and Harry Warfel, *Patterns of English* and *Understanding English,* new school and college texts by Paul Roberts, and the April 1956 and April 1958 issues of *The English Journal,* which are devoted to the teaching of language and grammar.

Encouraged by advances in teaching foreign language by the conversation, rather than the formal, method, modern scientific grammarians, the linguists, have made great progress in English-language teaching. They have emphasized that grammar is a means to an end rather than an end in itself. Their interest has been in how we do speak rather than in how it is thought we should speak.

Serious students of language have for many years been compiling data on the actual speech used in eight different areas of our country (New England, Middle Atlantic, South Atlantic, North Central, Upper Midwest, Rocky Mountain, Pacific Coast, and Louisiana), and their regional research projects comprise the tremendous work called *The Linguistic Atlas of the United States and Canada.* Through such careful study, a complete new direction of thought regarding language has been achieved. The work of the linguists in pointing out that differences in speech are mainly regional, not social, has encouraged friendliness, ease, and fluency in speech. It has discouraged superficial judgment of others by peculiarities of their language.

The linguists have shown that the rules by which we teachers grasped some pseudo-science of language are no longer worthy of being passed on to our students because they contain so many inconsistencies. According to Dr. Henry Lee Smith, Jr., "Grammatical rules are nothing more than the laying bare of the structure of the standard language as spoken and written congruously on varying levels in different culturally defined speech situations."[2] Applying scientific knowledge and reasoning, we now have an entirely new concept of grammar. There

[2] Letter of Henry Lee Smith, Jr., August 14, 1957.

has emerged a grammar of position, or word order, and a knowledge of the changing word forms and of the structure words that hold them together.

This change was inevitable when the proverbial pendulum swung too far in the direction of trying to apply pseudoscientific reasoning to language by a profusion of names for each of the various parts of speech until the student became so lost in the maze of grammatical nomenclature that practical application to language improvement was at a minimum. The first step toward making a change was to break faith with grammar as it was taught to us and as we were still teaching it. Men like Charles Carpenter Fries, Robert C. Pooley, John S. Kenyon, and others have illustrated that many old rules were untruthful and have stressed the historical approach to show how language changes have come about in the past and how current usage is bringing about changes today. Smith and George L. Trager have shown how the linguist applies method to his analysis. They point out how through metalinguistics, first outlined by B. L. Whorf, scientific conclusions can be reached correlating various speech usages with sociological facts concerning the speaker's social class, his status in the community, and the reactions of others to him.[3]

Studies made by Dr. Fries [4] show that out of every thousand different words that we might utter in simple sentences, 93 per cent can be grouped into four main classes. Because nomenclature can be confusing, these four main classes of words roughly correspond to, and can be designated by, our old familiar names of nouns, verbs, adjectives, and adverbs. All of the rest are just structure words. The four main classes are distinguished by their respective positions in the sentence. In contrast to the grammar of inflection, the grammar of position is easy to grasp.

[3] George L. Trager and Henry Lee Smith, Jr., *An Outline of English Structure* (Washington: American Council of Learned Societies, 1957), p. 83.

[4] Charles Carpenter Fries, *The Structure of English* (New York: Harcourt, Brace and Co., 1952).

Thus, English grammar now consists of three devices: word order, or position; structure or function words, and changing word forms. It is this last which is the bottomless pit over which the pendulum swings. Words change within themselves and in their endings, but the logic of why or how they change seems questionable. We cannot apply the old rules, and yet there are no new ones to take their place.

Here, fortunately, we see that the difficulties involved in learning our language are not ours alone but those of the language itself. Here we gain an appreciation of the many variations of the language acceptable in different regions of the country and the various levels of language used in any culture. We learn that language is a constantly changing process and that the variations in usage are right now bringing about changes.

Less fortunately, however, some of us may become so fascinated with the prospect of change that we think we should not presume to suggest any changes or corrections in a student's speech for fear we might upset the processes of the ages or embarrass him. We rationalize further that since so many different ways of saying the same thing are accepted by cultured people in different regions, who is to say what is correct in any case? We get so engrossed in tabulating the language peculiarities of the various regions that some think it will be a sorry day when there will be no more of these amusing peculiarities to tabulate. We forget we must focus attention on vocabulary enrichment and the development of a vivid and varied style in speaking and writing. Today too few students have sufficient training in these particular areas.

But must we go to extremes? Just because there is evidence to prove that a great many people say *off of*, particularly in our own regional area, doesn't mean that it isn't better to drop the superfluous word. True, many cultured speakers may use many such expressions; and it is comforting to know that; thanks to the work of the researchers, others are less critical. Because of the very personal nature of speech, however, one's own feeling of security in all types of situations is greatly dependent upon one's speech proficiency. Certain regularities, as well as the irregularities, do exist in our language even though it is unwise to try to lay down strict rules about them. To follow the regularities or to ignore them is not a moral issue of right and wrong, but a simple matter of better or poorer usage. Most of us are grateful for having had better forms pointed out to us along the way so that, as our thought matured, our language did also. If we came in contact with any teachers who were intolerant purists about English, we are not likely to charge them with having warped our personalities, and it is doubtful that even they could be impervious to the changing concept of language today.

There are those who warn that, in today's fashion, we must spare the verbal rod and be extremely cautious that we do not spoil the child by calling attention to any differences in so personal a thing as his language. At the same time, they say, as teachers, we must be overly conscious of our own terminology. We catch ourselves suggesting that differences or peculiarities could not possibly be errors. We think we must be careful of such terms as " levels of speech " because of the insinuation that some levels are lower than others. We may even feel that we need to use quotation marks when we say correct speech, for what we should mean is fashionable speech. We begin to wonder how far this attitude should go in view of the fact that the pendulum has already begun to swing back in regard to the usual meaning of spare the rod and spoil the child. (Spanking is now permissible again in many school systems, although the announcement will probably effect little change.)

The real question is, how far shall we let the pendulum swing in the direction of what many may interpret as a *laissez-faire* attitude regarding language? Now that the point has been made that expressions which may seem to be questionable in one area may be found to be used by cultured speakers in another area, how far are we to let this influence our effort to educate all American youth to the language patterns that are generally acceptable as standard American speech? To what extent shall we say, " There are no set standards " and " If it is communication, it is speech," and generally adopt the attitude that anything goes in speech as long as one is fluent? In this age of travel, are we to encourage provincialism as some sort of tourist attraction, or is it still our business as teachers to help enlighten all mankind? Is one who asks questions like these to be labeled a desk-bound purist or a die-hard grammarian?

Most English teachers today are neither desk-bound nor bookish purists. Because of the very nature of the subject matter they impart, they have had to stay in very close touch with the thoughts and interests of their students. Unconsciously, because they love boys and girls, or consciously to gain rapport, they use friendly, comfortable, informal speech on a level of mutual understanding. That does not say that the language is not basically correct according to good standards of informal usage, nor does it say that the present-day English teacher is averse to emitting a choice morsel of current " jive " when it will serve a good purpose in letting the class know that he is " hep."

" Desk-bound " can hardly be applied to today's high-school English teacher who rarely sits down in class unless it is with and beside his students, as they plan and execute the lesson. Today's teacher spends his vacations broadening his horizons and bringing back movies and slides to capture his memories and share them with others. Scholarly platitudes do not come readily to his lips, for his " leisure " hours are now filled with educational meetings and community work. Perhaps the teacher is also a homemaker with social, church, and club obligations. No, he's no longer bookish. The friendly, comfortable language of the people, disciplined by his educational and cultural background, comes easily to him, for instead of living in an ivory tower, he lives with the people and knows how to get along with them.

Such an English teacher does not treat students as " culpable transgressors" and begin to nag the minute he hears an expression that does not coincide with that of his own regional pattern. He knows better than to waste class time trying to instill the difference between *shall* and *will, It is I* or *It is me, further* or *farther*, and the split or unsplit infinitive if his students' pattern includes *I seen, I done,* and *we* and *you was.* Must I apologize for mentioning these last three items because, even though they were classed in the 1932 Sterling Andrus Leonard study as illiterate, they have been included in the *Atlas* worksheets? Surely not! Most of us do not have to go out of our own circle of friends to know that these expressions are used, but we can question how much their use contributes to a feeling of security in a cultured setting.

Conversely, we can also question what the textbooks say about the disputable items for which evidence is now available in the files of the *Atlas.* This is the subject of a 1958 doctoral dissertation at the University of Minnesota by Mrs. Jean Malmstrom of Western Michigan University titled *A Study of the Validity of Textbook Statements about Certain Controversial Grammatical Items in the Light of Evidence from the Linguistic Atlas.* It covers elementary, high school, and college textbooks from 1940 to 1955.

Should not the *Linguistic Atlas* reveal to us a need for more effective language teaching rather than suggest that one must not try to help students acquire fluency in a speech pattern that will be acceptable in the area where they hope to progress? Rather than to fear tampering with the provincial language because it is personal to the child, should we not build in him a feeling of awareness of, and regard for, the language inheritance which we all share? Surely we must not alter acceptable speech, but we can and must teach the use of good standard forms while bringing about awareness of the frequency and distribution of non-standard forms. We do not need to hop onto the pendulum and ride to its extremity. We can become enlightened to new viewpoints and temper them with common sense.

PART THREE

Remedial Lessons and Exercises

11 *The Presentation of a Unit on Language Structure*

In Chapters XI, XII, XIII, I shall attempt to suggest some of the types of lessons that should be stressed and to indicate a possible presentation of them. The language used is that which might actually be directed to the students. In other words, while reading these chapters, the teacher should visualize that he is presenting the lessons to a class.

INTRODUCTION TO THE LESSONS

To reiterate, new light has been focused upon the study of the English language. Now all that remains as true, consistent, and necessary to the science of language seems surprisingly simple. As Dr. Fries has shown, 93 per cent of every thousand different words that one might utter in a simple sentence can be grouped into four main classes, with the rest just structure words. Even though most of us are native-born speakers of the English language and need only to learn as much about it as will help us to use language more effectively, a new approach should make our study easier and far more enjoyable.

For our practical purpose, in line with scientific grammatical analysis, the four main word classes are simply—

I. Nouns (N.), II. Verbs (V.), III. Adjectives (ADJ.) and IV. Adverbs (ADV.).

	N.	V.		ADJ.	N.	ADV.
FOR EXAMPLE:	*John*	*wore*	*the*	*new*	*sweater*	*proudly.*

Our sentences consist mainly of arrangements of these four parts of speech. If we master them, we shall have mastered the feeling of what a sentence is. The work of the few remaining (structure) words in sentences and their use in developing variety will then be easily recognized.

Let us begin by reviewing these four all important parts of speech to see how they fit together into the utterances, or the sentences, we use.

LESSON I–NOUNS–CLASS I WORDS

Look again at the sentence:

N. V. ADJ. N. ADV.
John wore the new sweater proudly.

The word that fills the first main position in the sentence is *John.* This word, and any other name of a person, place or thing that we want to substitute for *John* is a NOUN. *Sweater* is also a noun because it, too, can be a first main position word as in " The sweater is red." What words may we substitute for *John?*

We can say: *Ann*
Mary
George
The baby *wore the new sweater proudly.*
The dog
My aunt
His sister
Mr. Jones

We can substitute any name of a person, place, or thing that would make sense. If we substituted other verbs for *wore* and other nouns for *sweater,* the list could be very long.

These words are nouns. They may be SINGULAR, indicating one (baby, dog), or PLURAL, indicating more than one (babies, dogs). They may have " signal " words like *the, a,* and *an* in front of them, and they may have other words (adjectives) that modify or change them. In any case, because they can stand in this first main position as the subject of the sentence, they are nouns. They may appear in other positions in the sentence (as the word *sweater* does above), but it is mainly because they can stand in the place of *John* in our sentence pattern that we consider them nouns.

NOUN SIGNALS:

(1) When *the,* or any word that could substitute for *the,* precedes a word, it is a signal that the word that follows is a noun. The noun will usually be a COMMON NOUN (name of *any* person, place, or thing).

The words that can substitute for *the* are called *markers* or *determiners* and are structure words. We shall call them DETERMINERS (D.).

D.	*N.*	D.	*N.*
The		A	
her		*an*	
his		*all*	
its		*any*	
many		*both*	
more		*few*	
one		*four*	
some		*five*	
that		*none*	
these			

(2) A capital letter is a signal that the word may be a PROPER NOUN (name of a *particular* person, place, or thing).

EXERCISE:

(1) Write lists of nouns under the following headings: *Common Nouns (Singular) Common Nouns (Plural) Proper Nouns*

(2) In the following sentences, identify the determiners by writing a D above them, the nouns by placing an N above them. (Remember that if a word could be moved to the first position and make sense there, it is a noun.)

1. *The lady took her child away.*
2. *My uncle loves all children.*
3. *Her record was broken.*
4. *The house has ten windows.*
5. *Both boys have books.*

(3) Make up at least five sentences. Label the determiners and the nouns.

PRONOUNS:

Pronouns (P.) are words that almost always take the place of nouns. They are structure words. Instead of *John* in the first main position in our original sentence, we could substitute these pronouns: *I, you, he, she, it, we, they,* or *who.* Because pronouns change form according to their position in the sentence, they will be studied later.

LESSON II—VERBS—CLASS II WORDS

The main position word is the SUBJECT or what we are speaking about. If we say this word, followed by the question *what?* we have found the second position word, the VERB. This word tells what *John* did or expresses action.

	N.	V.	D.	ADJ.	N.	ADV.
John *what*?	*John*	*wore*	*the*	*new*	*sweater*	*proudly.*
		showed				
		carried				
		held				

The list is limited only by the sense, and if there were substitutes for the words in the other positions, the sense would be unlimited.

John *what*? *John was*
did
cried
took

If we say the action word and then ask *who,* or *what,* as in " Who or what *took*? " we find the subject. (*John* took.)

Some verbs, like the verb *was,* express *being* rather than action.

Words that express action or being are VERBS.

The first main position word (noun) gives us the *simple subject,* and the second main word (verb) gives us the *simple predicate.* Together they form a simple sentence pattern: N. + V. or Subject + Predicate.

EXERCISE:

Make a short list of two-word sentences similar to the shortest one in the Bible: " Jesus wept."

DIRECT OBJECTS OF VERBS:

A word that receives or undergoes the action of a verb is called the DIRECT OBJECT.

N.	V.	N.
John	*wore*	*sweater.*
SUBJECT	VERB	OBJECT
(Who? or what?)	(does)	(what?)

N.	V.	N.
Mary	*writes*	*letters.*
SUBJECT	VERB	OBJECT
(Who? or what?)	(does)	(what?)

INDIRECT OBJECTS OF VERBS:

Do not confuse the person or thing undergoing or receiving the action with the person or thing to or for whom or which an action is performed.

N.	V.	N.	N.
Mary	*writes*	*John*	*letters.*
SUBJECT	VERB	IND. OBJ.	DIR. OBJ.
(Who? or what?)	(does)	(for whom?)	(what?)

In this sentence, *John,* to whom the letters are written, is the INDIRECT OBJECT.

EXERCISE:

Make up other four-word sentences following this pattern.

TENSE:

Verbs are not limited in time. Substitutes for the word *wore* in our original sentence may express present and future time and attitude as well as past time.

	PRESENT (Today or now)	PAST (Yesterday or last minute)	FUTURE (Tomorrow or next minute)
John	*tries*	*tried*	*will try*
He	*is*	*was*	*will be*
She	*takes*	*took*	*will take*
It	*does*	*did*	*will do*
	has	*had*	*will have*
	sits	*sat*	*will sit*
	shouts	*shouted*	*will shout*
	carries	*carried*	*will carry*
	inquires	*inquired*	*will inquire*
	examines	*examined*	*will examine*

AUXILIARIES:

Will and substitutes for *will* in the last column are called AUXILIARIES OR HELPERS (Aux.) and are structure words. They are not limited to future words or phrases. They include words or combinations of words such as *may, be, been, might, can, has, had, could, shall, would, should, must, is, was, did, got,* and *get.*

To form the future, or to state an action happening tomorrow or the next minute, we add Future Phrases to the general form of the present tense (but not to the special third person singular form ending in *s*; to *go,* for example, but not to *goes*).

VERB PHRASE:

The verb and all of its auxiliaries, or helpers, make up the VERB PHRASE (V. ph.). In recognizing a verb phrase in a sentence, be sure to find all of its auxiliaries.

EXAMPLE:

AUX.	V.
will have	*tried*
has been	*taken*
could have	*been*

EXERCISE:

In reading, the more rapidly your eye can span the structure words and find the basic meaning-carrying words of the sentence, the more rapidly you can read. See how quickly you can find and label subjects, complete verb phrases, direct and indirect objects in a set of exercise sentences or from a page in a book or magazine.

Make up sentences and label the parts. You may use them as a class exercise to test each other.

LESSON III – ADJECTIVES – CLASS III WORDS

Words that describe, qualify, or modify nouns and pronouns are ADJECTIVES. They may also limit or point out. Although they may be placed elsewhere, adjectives are words that can fit in position between *the* and the noun or after the verb.

D.	ADJ.	N.	V.	ADJ.	N.
The	*little*	*girl*	*writes*	*long*	*letters.*

D.	N.	V.	ADJ.
The	*sky*	*is*	*blue.*

P.	V.	ADJ.
He	*is*	*tall.*

SOUND TEST: Apply these questions to the noun or pronoun: How many? What kind (s)? Which one (s)? Whose? The answers that sound right will be ADJECTIVES.

EXAMPLES: Noun: *cow*

How many?—*one* cow
What kind?—*red Guernsey* cow
Which one?—*sad-faced* cow
Whose?—*John's* cow
Whose?—*his* cow

Note: Possessive words are adjectives when they do the work of adjectives. These include *Mary's, Bob's, my, your, his, her, its, our,* and *their.*

EXERCISE:

(1) Make up separate sentences in which you use each of the following words as a noun, a verb, and an adjective: *hand, star, rope, guard.* Label the sentence parts you have learned.

(2) The words with which we paint pictures are adjectives. See how many colorful substitutes you can find for our most common and overworked adjectives such as *little, old, pretty.* Perhaps each student could take a different adjective and make up a list of substitutes.

LESSON IV – ADVERBS – CLASS IV WORDS

Words that tell *how, when,* or *where* about the verbs are ADVERBS. They can be placed in the position following the other three main words but may be used elsewhere in the sentence.

SOUND TEST: Say the verb and ask in turn: How? When? Where? The answer will give you the ADVERB, if there is one.

EXAMPLES:

D.	ADJ.	N.	V.	ADV.	
The	*little*	*child*	*danced*	*gracefully.*	Danced how?
The	*little*	*child*	*danced*	*yesterday.*	Danced when?
The	*little*	*child*	*danced*	*out.*	Danced where?

Most adverbs are formed by adding *ly* to an adjective.

ADJECTIVES	ADVERBS
bright	*brightly*
cheerful	*cheerfully*
confident	*confidently*
frequent	*frequently*
glad	*gladly*
happy	*happily*
immediate	*immediately*
noisy	*noisily*
polite	*politely*
separate	*separately*

NOTE: Not all words ending in *ly*, however, are adverbs. *Lonely* is an adjective. *Kindly* may be an adjective depending upon its use. *Very* and words which could substitute for the word *very* are also classed as adverbs. These could be called DEGREE (Deg.) words because, like the word *very*, they are structure words that show degree, extent, or power.

EXAMPLES:

P.	V.	DEG.	ADJ.
She	*is*	*very*	*pretty.*
		quite	
		really	
		even	
		still	
		somewhat	

P.	V.	DEG.	ADV.
He	*walked*	*very*	*slowly.*
		terribly	
		extremely	
		unusually	
		more	
		so	

As can be seen here, degree words qualify or modify either adjectives or adverbs. Adverbs, the last of the four main classes of words, then, include " pure " adverbs (Class IV words) and degree or structure words.

DEFINITION: Words, including degree words, which modify verbs, adjectives, and other adverbs are ADVERBS.

EXERCISE:

Identify and label the adjectives and adverbs in a list of practice sentences or a printed page.

SUMMARY:

(1) Nouns, verbs, adjectives, and adverbs are now sometimes referred to as Class I, Class II, Class III, and Class IV words.

(2) The position of the word in the sentence and its relation to the other words determines its class name or part of speech.

(3) We have now learned the basic elements of the sentence. To gain facility in language, however, we need to know the function of the few remaining structure words and how they work together to express our ideas.

LESSON V – PREPOSITIONS

At and words that can be substituted for *at* in a sentence are called prepositions. These include *to, in, on, under, around, with, of, above, between, among,* etc.

The PREPOSITION (Prep.) is a signal that a noun or pronoun, perhaps both, are coming after it.

Only certain pronouns come after prepositions. They are the same as those which come after verbs. It may require thought in choosing the acceptable one, especially when the preposition has more than one word after it.

EXAMPLES of pronouns used after prepositions as objects:

PREP.	PRONOUNS	PREP.	NOUNS AND PRONOUNS		
with	*me*	*above*	*John*	*and*	*him*
in	*him*	*behind*	*Mary*	*and*	*her*
for	*us*	*over*	*you*	*and*	*me*
by	*her*	*after*	*it*	*and*	*them*
around	*them*	*upon*	*the car*	*and*	*us*
to	*whom*	*between*	*them*	*and*	*us*

The group of words, as above, introduced by the preposition and ending with a noun or a pronoun is called a PREPOSITIONAL PHRASE. Prepositional phrases generally do the work of, and can be substituted for, adjectives and adverbs.

LESSON VI – PRONOUNS

As defined in Lesson I words that almost always take the place of nouns are PRONOUNS. All but two pronouns referring to persons (*you* and *it*) and the indefinite ones (*which, that, what*) change their forms according to their position in the sentence and, therefore, require study. We can forget about *you* and *it* and those that don't change, but good speakers and writers are careful in their choice of the forms of the others.

NOMINATIVE OR SUBJECTIVE	OBJECTIVE
BEFORE–PRONOUNS	AFTER–PRONOUNS
(Before the verb in statements)	(After the verb and after prepositions)
I	*me*
we	*us*
he	*him*
she	*her*
they	*them*
who	*whom*
whoever	*whomever*

MEMORY TRICK:

Before–pronoun	After–pronoun
I — *we*	
he — *she*	The others
they — *who*	

HOW PRONOUNS WORK:

BEFORE THE VERB		AFTER THE VERB		AFTER THE PREPOSITION
I		*me*		*me.*
We		*us*		*us.*
He	gave	*him*	to	*him.*
She		*her*		*her.*
They		*them*		*them.*
Who		*whom*		*whom?*

SOUND TEST: When there are two words for the same position, try the sound of each separately. Trust your sense of sound by the omission test.

CAUTION: (1) Use only the Before-pronouns as subjects.

(2) Use only the After-pronouns as objects of verbs or after prepositions.

EXCEPTIONS: The verb *to be* takes Before-pronouns on *both* sides in formal writing and speaking.

EXAMPLES: *It* is *I*. *She* was *he* in the play. John and *he* could have been *they*.

These pronouns, called PERSONAL PRONOUNS, are said to be in the first, second, or third person depending upon whether the pronoun indicates

(1) the person speaking (first person)
(2) the person spoken to (second person)
(3) the person or thing spoken of (third person)

PRONOUN CHART:

	NOMINATIVE OR SUBJECTIVE (Before-pronoun)		OBJECTIVE (After-pronoun)	
Person	Singular	Plural	Singular	Plural
1st (speaking)	*I*	*we*	*me*	*us*
2nd (spoken to)	*you*	*you*	*you*	*you*
3rd (spoken of)	*he, she, it*	*they*	*him, her, it*	*them*

If you know this chart, you will be able to communicate with others about language by being able to designate any pronoun you wish. Memorize it. Most people do. (Third person singular pronouns are identified as *masculine, feminine,* and *neuter.*)

EXERCISE:

(1) Play a class game in which you call for certain pronouns by person and number.

(2) Make up sentences using pronouns. In oral class drill call on another student to choose the correct pronoun.

LESSON VII – ING WORDS AND INFINITIVES

(1) *Ing* words are made by adding *ing* to the present tense form of a verb.

(2) A word group consisting of the preposition *to* and the present form of a verb is called an INFINITIVE.

(3) An infinitive is always used when we wish to refer to a verb by name. We speak of a verb as the verb *to do* or the verb *to be,* etc. *Ing* words and infinitives may introduce phrases.

ING WORDS		INFINITIVES	
(verb + *ing*)		(*to* + verb)	
go	*ing*	*to*	*go*
say	*ing*	*to*	*say*
do	*ing*	*to*	*do*

ING WORDS AS PHRASES	INFINITIVES AS PHRASES
going home	to go away
saying a prayer	to say a prayer
doing homework	to do homework

ING WORDS AND INFINITIVES, either alone or as phrases, may do the work of nouns, of adjectives, or of adverbs. *The,* or another determiner, before an *ing* word is the signal that the *ing* word is a substitute for a noun. If it, or its phrase, stands instead of the first position word in the sentence, it is doing the work of a noun. If it modifies a verb, it is doing the work of an adverb.

EXERCISE:

In sentences, underline the *ing* words and infinitives (single words and complete phrases) and write above them a symbol to show the kind of work they do in the sentence. Use a page from a newspaper or magazine.

REVIEW: Subjects and objects are nouns. They may come before the verb or after verbs and propositions.

Words that modify or describe nouns and pronouns are adjectives.

Words that modify verbs, adjectives, or other adverbs are adverbs.

LESSON VIII – CONJUNCTIONS AND CLAUSE WORDS

AND and IF:

Two important structure words, *and* and *if,* provide the means by which we combine our thoughts into varied and interesting sentences.

And and substitutes for *and,* called CONJUNCTIONS (Conj.), are used to join two parts. They may join two words, two groups of words, two sentences, or they may connect a series of any of these.

Conjunctions can best be remembered by this little rhyme:

And, or, nor,
But, yet, for.

They may connect two simple sentences to form a COMPOUND SENTENCE.

A simple sentence + a simple sentence = a compound sentence.

N. V. *and* N. V.
or
nor
but
yet
for

If and substitutes for *if* provide the means by which we introduce a subordinate or dependent (leaner, crutch) thought into the sentence. They include all the words that stand in the position of *if* in the following sentence:

The boy will be happy *if* the sun shines.
If the sun shines, the boy will be happy.
The boy, *if* the sun shines, will be happy.

Substitutes for *if* include *after, when, whenever, since, because, although,* and *while.* Since *if* and substitutes for *if* introduce a group containing a subject and a verb, we call them CLAUSE WORDS (Cl.). Because of the presence of the clause word, the complete clause cannot stand alone and is said to be dependent or subordinate. Such a clause changes a simple sentence into an expanded or COMPLEX SENTENCE.

PHRASES AND CLAUSES:

Groups of words may be added to the sentence to do the work of one of the four main classes of words: nouns, verbs, adjectives, or adverbs. These groups of words are either phrases or clauses. The difference between them is this: A CLAUSE contains a subject and a verb. A PHRASE does not.

PHRASES may be:

(1) Prepositional (*at the door*)
(2) *Ing* word (*singing* the song)
(3) Infinitive (*to go* home)

Any number of phrases may be added to a simple sentence, and it will still be a simple sentence. When a dependent clause is added, the sentence is no longer simple; it is complex.

CLAUSE SIGNALS:

The following words serve as signals to tell us that a clause will follow:

NOUN AND ADJECTIVE CLAUSE SIGNALS	ADVERB CLAUSE SIGNALS
who	*after*
whom	*when*
which	*if*
that	*since*
how	*before*
when	*because*
where	*although*
what	*while*

Some noun and adjective clause signals, besides being connecting words, may serve as subjects or objects in their own clauses. Whether to use *who* or *whom* causes some confusion. It depends on the use of the word within the clause.

SOUND TEST: Give *who* and *whom* the *he* and *him* sound test. If you can substitute *he*, use *who*; if you can substitute *him*, use *whom*.

EXERCISE:

Make up sentences in which you use each of the clause signals listed above.

LESSON IX – INTERJECTIONS AND SENTENCES

A gesture or a single word may express an idea. We communicate meaning with the single word, "Go!" just as we convey the same meaning with a motion of the hand. A single word, then, may be considered a sentence.

Verbs, as single words, may express statements, commands, or questions. INTERJECTIONS, which are single-word expressions of strong feeling, may convey a variety of emotions; such words are *oh! amen! golly!* and *whoopee!* One professor[1] has collected more than 500 of these little words. They may be attached to a sentence if they express mild feeling or may stand alone if they express strong feeling.

KINDS OF SENTENCES:

For our purpose of learning to express ourselves more effectively in speaking and thus in writing, we shall start with the two-word sentence which contains a noun and a verb. By a simple formula given below we shall learn to recognize three main kinds of sentences according to their grammatical structure: simple, complex, and compound.

	N.	V.	N.	V.	N.
1. SIMPLE	*Birds*	*fly.*	*Boy*	*meets*	*girl.*

	N.	V.	ADV.	CL.	D.	N.	V.
2. COMPLEX	*Birds*	*fly*	*south*	*when*	*the*	*leaves*	*fall.*

	N.	V.	ADV.	PREP.	N.	CONJ.	P.
3. COMPOUND	*Birds*	*fly*	*south*	*in*	*winter,*	*and*	*they*

V.	PREP.	D.	N.
return	*in*	*the*	*spring.*

One complete thought expressed by a subject and a predicate forms a simple sentence.

[1] Clyde Crobaugh, University of Tennessee, "Haw, What a Hobby!" *Colliers,* CXXXVII, no. 5 (March 2, 1956), 48-49.

One thought with one or more dependent thoughts added forms a complex sentence.

Two or more complete and independent thoughts joined form a compound sentence.

SENTENCE FORMULAS:

Simple—N. V.	(1)	One thought.
Complex—N. V. + *N. V.*	($1\frac{1}{2}$)	One thought and one dependent thought or more.
Compound—N. V. + N. V.	(1 + 1)	One thought, *and* one thought.

By using different kinds of sentences, we make speech and writing interesting.

EXERCISE:

Make up practice sentences, containing phrases and clauses. Enclose the phrases and clauses in parentheses. Indicate the kinds of work they do in the sentences by writing *noun, verb, adjective,* or *adverb* above each phrase or clause. At the end of each sentence, write the kind of sentence it is (simple, complex, or compound).

LESSON X—MORE ABOUT VERBS

NOTE TO THE TEACHER: The following lesson may be omitted. It is included here because of the tendency on the part of the students for whom this work has been undertaken to omit all auxiliaries. Students who do not hear auxiliaries for imitation may need purposely to study them. Classing all of them simply as substitutes for *will* does not suffice to show which ones to use in certain situations.

ACTIVE AND PASSIVE VOICE:

When the subject performs the action, the verb is said to be in the ACTIVE VOICE:

PRESENT		PAST		FUTURE
(Today, this minute)		(Yesterday, the last minute)		(Tomorrow, the next minute)
Singular	Plural	Singular	Plural	
I take *I'm taking*	*we take* *we're taking*	*I took* *I did take*	*we took* *we did take*	Present tense with future phrases:
you take *you're taking*	*you take* *you're taking*	*you took* *you did take*	*you took* *you did take*	*shall, will,* or *'ll take;* or
he takes *he's taking*	*they take* *they're taking*	*he took* *he did take*	*they took* *they did take*	*shall be, will be,* or *'ll be taking*

When the subject is acted upon, the verb is in the PASSIVE VOICE:

PRESENT		PAST	
Singular	Plural	Singular	Plural
I am taken	*we are taken*	*I was taken*	*we were taken*
you are taken	*you are taken*	*you were taken*	*you were taken*
he is taken	*they are taken*	*he was taken*	*they were taken*

FUTURE

Main verb of the passive voice preceded by

shall be, will be, or *'ll be*

TENSE FORMS:

Besides the present and past tenses and future phrases given above, there are present perfect, past perfect, and future perfect phrases, which indicate action having been completed or perfected, at the time expressed, as shown below.

(In the passive voice, the perfect forms employ both the verb *to be* and the verb *to have* as auxiliaries.)

PASSIVE VOICE PERFECT PHRASES

Present Perfect Phrases

I have been taken	*we have been taken*
you have been taken	*you have been taken*
he has been taken	*they have been taken*

Past Perfect Phrases

I had been taken	*we had been taken*
you had been taken	*you had been taken*
he had been taken	*they had been taken*

Future Perfect Phrases

Shall, will, or *'ll* added to the present perfect verb and suxiliary:

I shall have been taken

If we drop the word *taken* from all of the forms above, we have the conjugation of the verb *to be.*

CONTRACTIONS:

In informal speech contractions like *'ve* and *'d* (*I've, I'd*) are most frequently used. Conjugate verbs aloud using the contracted forms of *I've, you've, I'd, you'd, I'll, you'll,* etc.

PRINCIPAL PARTS OF VERBS:

How do we know when to say *take* and when to say *taken*? If we constantly hear the better form, we will say it from imitation. Those who do not hear it and do not say it, need to study a list of the three principal parts of verbs. Many people memorize this list, shown below, to the extent that if given the first part, they can quickly say the other two parts.

PRESENT TENSE (*Today I—*)	PAST TENSE (*Yesterday I—*)	PAST PARTICIPLE (*I have—*)
add	*added*	*added*
am (not *be*)	*was*	*been*
go	*went*	*gone*
do	*did*	*done*
take	*took*	*taken*
sing	*sang*	*sung*
drink	*drank*	*drunk*
throw	*threw*	*thrown*
run	*ran*	*run*

PRESENT TENSE (*Today I—*)	PAST TENSE (*Yesterday I—*)	PAST PARTICIPLE (*I have—*)
wear	*wore*	*worn*
speak	*spoke*	*spoken*
ride	*rode*	*ridden*
write	*wrote*	*written*
come	*came*	*come*
lay	*laid*	*laid*
lie	*lay*	*lain*
sit	*sat*	*sat*
set	*set*	*set*
choose	*chose*	*chosen*
creep	*crept*	*crept*
say	*said*	*said*
swim	*swam*	*swum*
swing	*swung*	*swung*

LEARN THIS PRINCIPLE:

The present tense and future phrases are built upon the words in the first column.

The simple past is the middle column.

The forms of the perfect precede the words of the third column.

EXERCISE:

(1) Make up drill sentences for practice in choosing the best form of the verb. Read your sentences and ask others to identify and give the tense of your verb phrases.

(2) Chant the principal parts aloud together, noting particularly the past participle.

LESSON XI – REVIEW CHART

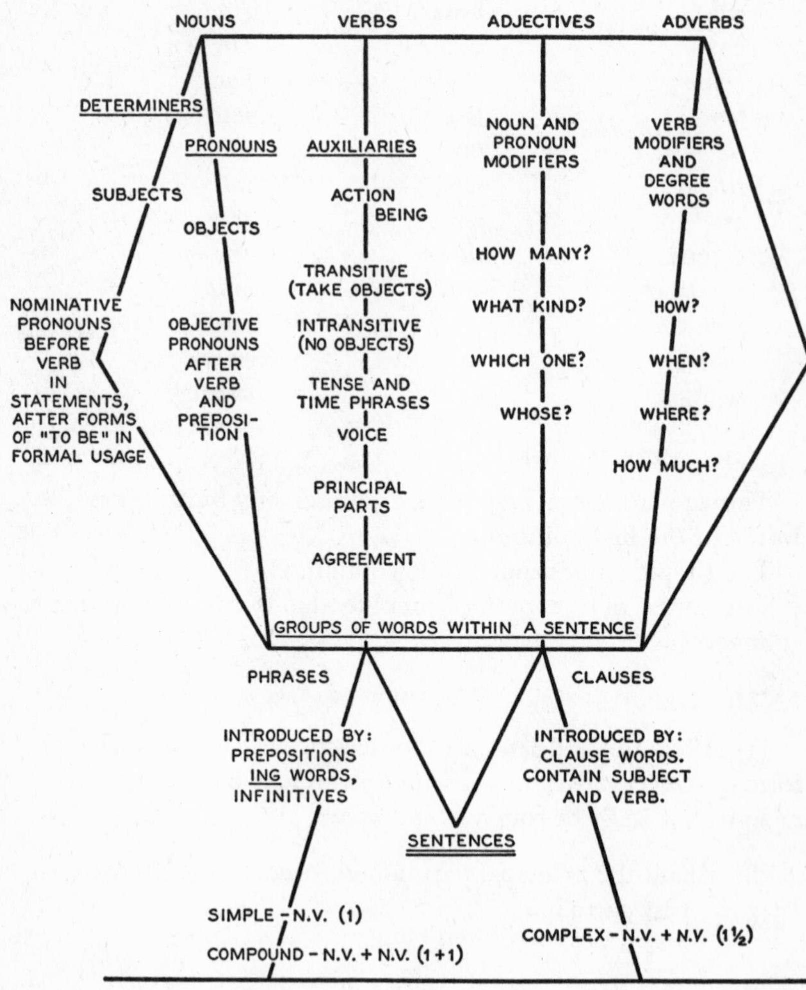

12 *Good Usage*

TO TEACHERS: As in the preceding chapter, I am attempting here to suggest types of lessons that are needed and to show by example a possible presentation of them. They may be duplicated or copied for actual use in class.

The study of language is of little value unless we put what we learn into practice to improve our speech and our writing. A big part of education is the process of change. We are constantly changing old habits into better ones. Students should practice good usage in speech until it becomes habit, and soon old, worn-out forms will sound unusual to them.

Common errors in the use of verbs usually involve: tense forms, omission of auxiliaries, agreement with the subject.

LESSON I – I SAW and I DID

The verb *to see* deserves study because many people substitute *seen* for *saw* in the past tense.

PRESENT TENSE		PAST TENSE	
I see	*we see*	*I saw*	*we saw*
you see	*you see*	*you saw*	*you saw*
he sees	*they see*	*he saw*	*they saw*

PRESENT PERFECT PHRASES		PAST PERFECT PHRASES	
I've seen	*we've seen*	*I'd seen*	*we'd seen*
you've seen	*you've seen*	*you'd seen*	*you'd seen*
he's seen	*they've seen*	*he'd seen*	*they'd seen*

Now go back over these forms substituting *do* for *see, did* for *saw,* and *done* for *seen.*

In class, practice repeating the past tense around the room rapidly, each one adding a different object to complete the questions, *I saw what?* and *I did what?* Time yourselves to see how much faster you can do it the second time.

If you are one who says, "*I seen it*" and "*I done it,*" break the habit now before it becomes more firmly fixed. Drill yourself on the acceptable form until it becomes automatic. Listen for it in your speech and in that of others. When you hear yourself saying the better form automatically, then you can start working on another questionable speech habit.

TROUBLESOME PAIRS:

The following verbs are often confused in meaning as well as in tense. Try substituting them for the verb *to see* above.

Lie – to rest or recline
Lay – to put or place something

Sit – to rest the bottom of the body on the top of a seat
Set – to put or place something

Learn – to get knowledge
Teach – to give instruction

Bring – to indicate motion toward the speaker
Take – to indicate motion away from the speaker

Let – to allow or permit
Leave – to go away from

Rise – to get up or to go up
Raise – to lift something

Borrow – to have the temporary use of
Lend – to give the temporary use of

Can – to be able
May – to have permission

EXERCISE:

Make up sentences using these forms correctly. Play a game in class in which a student reads a sentence substituting *bebop* for the word in question and calls on someone else to give the word he wants.

LESSON II – "ED," A SIGNAL OF THE PAST TENSE

Most of our past tense verbs end in *ed, d,* or *t.* Sometimes *ed* and *d* endings are pronounced with a voiced *d* sound, and sometimes with a voiceless *t* sound. Say the sounds several times and notice where your tongue ends and remains after each sound. Many people who don't enunciate clearly fail to give this past tense signal any quality at all. It is easy to understand, then, why they leave it off in writing.

EXERCISE:

(1) So that you may become more aware of the *d* and *t* sounds as past tense signals, write two columns of verbs. In the first column, list all of the verbs that are pronounced with a voiceless *t* sound at the end no matter how the ending may be spelled. In the second column, list those that are given the voiced *d* sound at the end. Omit the verbs that you think could go in either column.

EXAMPLE:

t	*d*
skipped	*cried*
crept	*decided*
liked	*advised*
announced	*agreed*

(2) Many past tense verbs do not end in *ed.* Some of these are:

knew (never *knowed*)
burst (never *busted*)
caught (never *catched*)

See how many you can add to this list. Use them in sentences.

(3) Make a long list of verbs that could be substituted for *walked*. Do the same for *said* and for other overworked words.

EXAMPLES:

walked	said
ambled	*answered*
cavorted	*asserted*
dragged	*blurted*
eased	*bragged*
hurried	*chuckled*

LESSON III – TROUBLESOME PERFECT FORMS

Verbs in the third or last column of the three principal parts are the ones with which we express action completed or perfected. To do so, we must use auxiliary or helping verbs like those in the left column below. To express perfect phrases, the words on the right, below, must have before them one of the words from the left column. Some perfect forms, however, are the same as their present or past tense forms (*brought, burst, caught*). If used without the helping verb, they may express present or past tense.

AUXILIARY VERBS (Signals for the main verb)	PERFECT FORMS (These must have helpers)
have	*beaten*
has	*been*
had	*begun*
is	*bitten*
was	*blown*
were	*broken*
am	*chosen*

AUXILIARY VERBS (Signals for the main verb)	PERFECT FORMS (These must have helpers)
am being	*done*
is being	*drawn*
are	*drunk*
are being	*eaten*
was being	*flown*
were being	*frozen*
shall be	*given*
will be	*gone*
should be	*lain*
could be	*rung*
might be	*raised*
can be	*seen*
having been	*sung*
had been	*spoken*
could have been	*shaken*
should have been	*sprung*
may have been	*taken*
might have been	*written*

The most common misuse in regard to this principle occurs with the following words: *seen, done, come, taken,* and *written.* Do not put a pronoun (I or he) before them without a helper.

EXERCISE:

Write sentences using the perfect phrases. Exchange papers and read each other's, checking spelling, capitalization, and end punctuation, as well as the verbs.

LESSON IV – OMISSION OF AUXILIARY VERBS

The omission of the auxiliary verbs is one of the three most common verb troubles. We have seen that we must not omit the auxiliary verbs if we wish to indicate the perfect phrases.

Other common omissions occur when the present tense is

expressed in its *ing* form. Here the forms of the verb *to be* must be clearly heard.

PRESENT TENSE

I am going	*we are going*	*I'm going*	*we're going*
you are going	*you are going*	*you're going*	*you're going*
he is going	*they are going*	*he's going*	*they're going*

Careless speakers often omit the helping word *do* in a question like: *What do you mean? What do you say?*

Sometimes forms of the verb *to be* are omitted when they are the main verb. You must not omit the main verb in such sentences as:

What are you doing?
He is absent.
What is your high school?
She is very happy.
Now you are talking.
He is old enough.
You are coming, aren't you?
You are going, I hear.
Who is there?

EXERCISE:

Try writing a few sentences or a little story in which you use as many as possible of the above sentences or ones like them. Take turns reading them to the class.

LESSON V — AGREEMENT OF SUBJECT AND VERB

Another difficulty many people have with verbs has to do with matching the right verb form with the subject. Certain verbs and subjects " agree " or " go together." They must not be confused if one wants to use effective language. The most frequent cause of confusion concerns the placement of the final *s* sound of the verb.

EXERCISE:

Write the headings: NOUNS and VERBS at the top of a page. Write under NOUNS some singular and some plural first position words (names of persons, places, or things). Under VERBS write a corresponding list of words expressing action happening as of now (present tense).

Draw a circle around every final *s* on your page. Note that with nouns, this final letter *s* represents plural. With verbs, the final *s* represents singular. Note, also, that if there is an *s* at the end of a word in your noun column, there will not be one opposite it in the verb column.

EXAMPLES:

Nouns	Verbs
Boy	*does*
Boys	*do*
Girl	*has*
Girls	*have*

Study this principle you have illustrated. Nouns and present tense verbs form their plurals in opposite ways. Read your lists aloud to attune your ears to good usage.

The nouns (or subjects) and verbs *agree* because both must be singular or both must be plural, but by *agreeing*, they *look* like opposites. In the present tense:

(1) With a name and with *he, she,* or *it,* put the final *s* on the verb.

(2) Do not put the final *s* on a verb used with *I, you, we,* or *they.*

Say	Do not say
John likes.	*I likes.*
He is.	*You is.*
She goes.	*We goes.*
It gives.	*They gives.*

USAGE GAME:

Take turns around the room rapidly with one person saying a noun or pronoun not previously given, and the next person saying a present tense verb that has not previously been given. Two or three people, who do not need the drill, could volunteer to stand as listeners and referees. Anyone who hesitates too long, misplaces an *s* sound, or repeats a word, must rest an elbow on the desk and hold up a hand. After his two hands are up, he is out of the game and must stand.

PRACTICE THESE ORAL VERB DRILLS:

The following pronoun order gives emphasis to the third person singular where the most difficulty lies. New order requires thought, and thought must accompany repetition for it to be meaningful and beneficial.

to see	to go	to like
I see.	*I go.*	*I like.*
You see.	*You go.*	*You like.*
Who sees?	*Who goes?*	*Who likes?*
He sees.	*He goes.*	*He likes.*
She sees.	*She goes.*	*She likes.*
It sees.	*It goes.*	*It likes.*
John sees.	*John goes.*	*John likes.*
We see.	*We go.*	*We like.*
They see.	*They go.*	*They like.*

to be	to do	to have
I am.	*I do.*	*I have*
You are.	*You do.*	*You have.*
Who is?	*Who does?*	*Who has?*
He is.	*He does.*	*He has.*
She is.	*She does.*	*She has.*
It is.	*It does.*	*It has.*
John is.	*John does.*	*John has.*
We are.	*We do.*	*We have.*
They are.	*They do.*	*They have.*

Practice the same oral drill substituting other words such as: *to mean, to love, to hit, to bring, to take, to sit, to help, to try, to make, to eat.* Change the order of the middle group occasionally or add objects to the verbs.

EXERCISE:

(1) Strike out the wrong form of the verb in each sentence. Then read the sentences aloud. If you have trouble with agreement, practice reading them over and over.

1. The book, *Cress Delahanty,* (consist, consists) of a series of short stories that (take, takes) Cress Delahanty from her twelfth year to her sixteenth.
2. One critic (describe, describes) Miss West's style in these stories as " wry, compassionate comedy."
3. Some stories, like the tale of the huge hat burdened with fruits and flowers which Cress bought to catch Edwin's attention, (turn, turns) to broad comedy.
4. Others are gently thoughtful, like the one in which her grandfather's hired man (try, tries) to explain that her grandfather (feel, feels) his wife's death keenly, though Cress (think, thinks) he is just being cantankerous.
5. Cress (go, goes) to visit a girl named Ina who (need, needs) Cress to help make her reputation in school.
6. Cress (don't, doesn't) want to go because she (know, knows) Ina's father (read, reads) long chapters of the Bible before every meal.
7. He (make, makes) Cress read a chapter that (has, have) words she (know, knows) she can utter only because they are in the Good Book.
8. Then he (take, takes) her for a walk after supper, and she (has, have) to stand by while he (drown, drowns) a snake slowly in an oil pool by pushing it back each time it (tries, try) to escape.
9. He (seem, seems) to her so brutal and horrible that she

(escape, escapes) and (walk, walks) all the way home to the ranch that night.

10. Other stories (cover, covers) phases of growing up that have to do with competing for the debating team because her idol is captain, what she (do, does) when her complexion is spotty, how she (avoid, avoids) bad luck, and how she (live, lives) through her infatuation for an older man.

(2) Pretend you are a radio announcer giving an on-the-spot description of some exciting and unusual event such as an earthquake, a flood, a fire, a sports event, a descent of Martians, an atomic explosion, or something less exciting such as what your classmates are doing at the moment, a school assembly, or a dance.

Whenever possible, use present tense verbs of the *he runs* form rather than *he is running.*

Volunteers might give a few impromptu examples before the class prepares carefully written and condensed examples to be read, tape recorded, and played back for listening.

LESSON VI – DOUBLE NEGATIVES and "BE" TROUBLE

Two common speech habits which are now old-fashioned and suggest that the user isn't alert are the double negative and the misuse of the word *be.*

No, not, n't are negatives. Use only one negative in a sentence. Do not use a negative with *hardly* or *but* in sentences like: *He can hardly lift his arm* and *He can but try.*

Be is a perfectly good word, but is misused and overworked. If you can substitute *is* or *are* for *be,* do so.

EXERCISE:

(1) Make up sentences in which you use negatives correctly. Practice reading them aloud.

(2) Listen for sentences in which *be* is used. Decide if the

usage is good, or if there is a different way of saying the same thing, as in *He don't be here,* which you would change to *He isn't here.*

LESSON VII – GOOD USAGE PATTERNS

EXERCISE:

(1) Practice the following correct forms until they are a part of your speech pattern. Record them on tape, leaving time for repetition on the play-back, or divide them into pairs and practice reading the drills to each other.

1. I'm not; you aren't; he isn't; we aren't; you aren't; they aren't.
2. This boy; this man; this chair; that girl; that book; that pencil.
3. That's mine; people are; men are; women are; anyway; nowhere; anywhere; everywhere; somewhere.
4. I can't go since I was out late last night. I voted for her because she speaks well.
5. He isn't here; she isn't here; they aren't here; he's absent.
6. It doesn't matter whether he ought or ought not to go. I ought to go.
7. I don't have any, and he doesn't have any. Do you have some?
8. This is as far as I can go. That is as far as I can tell.
9. Regardless of the price, it is not secondhand furniture.
10. Do you remember? I forget. Did you forget too? I knew it yesterday.
11. I did it; I saw it; I took it. We did it; we saw it; we took it.
12. I brought my book; I brought my paper; I brought my pencil.
13. I saw the picture; he saw the picture; we saw the picture.
14. He doesn't; she doesn't; it doesn't. Doesn't he? Doesn't she? Doesn't it?

15. He might have; he could have; she should have; I would have; I must have.
16. Between John and me; between Mary and her; between them and us.
17. She taught me to draw cartoons. Will you please teach me to paint?
18. We were going; we were walking; we were talking. Were we doing it right?
19. You were saying; you were asking; you were there. Were you going? Were you there?
20. They were coming; they were going; they were there. Were they ready? Were they there?
21. She says she has; he says he has. She goes; she walks; she takes; she works.
22. She's at home. You are wrong. They're gone. He's well. It is taken. He isn't here.
23. He took her; she took him; I took him; you took her; we took them; they took him.
24. I help her; she helps them; we helped them; you helped him; they helped her.
25. He asked if I would go. I asked if she would go. They asked if we would go.

(2) For drill on troublesome sounds, find and practice some good tongue twisters. Fred Allen called them " phrases that get your tang all tongueled up." (See Chapter 13, Lesson II.)

LESSON VIII – STUPID STORIES

What are your particular usage problems? Why not discuss them in class and try writing some little " Stupid Stories " for oral drill like the examples below? If each one reads his story containing the good usage he wishes to emphasize, his ears will soon become attuned to more effective language.

EXAMPLES:

Take Your Pick. You may take your pick of the pictures. I

drew a picture of a cream pitcher, but the picture I drew looks more like a picture of a vase than a picture of a cream pitcher. I drew a picture of a baseball pitcher, and this picture is better than my picture of a cream pitcher. Which picture will you pick?

The Little Rat Named Kite. Once there was a little rat named Kite who liked to fight. He didn't know why, so he would lie. He tried with all his might to get into my high school, but every door was too tight. He tried and tried every night until it was light, but he couldn't find an opening that was just right. He couldn't bite his way to make it right because he had lost both front teeth in a fight. He was a sorry sight. All he could do was sigh and wonder why. Perhaps it was right that the little rat named Kite found the doors so tight that he couldn't squeeze in with all his might, for at my high school you can't stay if you like to lie and fight.

EXERCISE:

(1) If you wish to improve your speech, try writing some "*Stupid Stories*" suggested by the following titles, frequently using words containing the diphthong as in *bite*:

Too Fat to Fight
The Icicles on the Island
Highty-Flighty
A Mighty Mite

(2) Practice reading this little story:

Mr. Pike and His Kite. Mr. Pike likes to exercise with his kite. Everytime the mighty kite climbs the clouds, Mr. Pike cries with delight. Although he is an odd type and like a child, Mr. Pike is very nice, and everyone likes him. It is not a crime to like to play with kites. It is a sign that one can enjoy life even in its prime.

(3) Take turns reading the following sentences aloud or

use them with the listen-and-repeat technique *via* the tape recorder.

1. What time did he arrive?
2. Were you surprised to see Clyde?
3. He said he tried to call you five times.
4. Why do I sigh? I know speech usage isn't a matter of right or wrong. It's just of a higher or lower quality.
5. It is time to arrive at this conclusion: I must try to take more pride in my speech.
6. It is time to be wise and pry into my reactions.
7. I realize why it is better to use speech that seems right for high-school students in this area.
8. I recognize that when I am criticized, it is for my own good.
9. Through exercise, I can rise and shine in speech as well as in everything else I do.
10. I shall open my mouth wide to say *i* as in *bite*.

If you have been saying *rat* when you mean *right,* changing this one sound may be the key to changing your entire speech pattern to a more effective one. By focusing attention on this one sound, you will begin to hear your own speech as others hear it, and you may automatically change other purely regional pronunciations and expressions to the standard and universally accepted forms. New vistas will be opened to you as your speech measures up to your opportunities.

(4) Make up a long list of words containing the diphthong as in *cry, tie,* and *reply.* Practice reading it every day. Listen for these words in your own speech and in that of others.

CHORAL READING:

For choral reading in class try "The Highwayman" by Alfred Noyes. In addition to the two male solo lines, work out interesting effects by designating certain lines to certain pitch groups. To form the pitch groups, each student could say in turn, " The Lord is my Shepherd," after which the teacher could assign him to one of the following groups: girls high, girls low, boys high, boys low, depending upon the pitch of the voice. Then the students could change seats so that those with voices of similar pitch would sit together.

Students should be careful to use a good diphthong in the words *highwayman* and *riding* and also be careful to follow the leader so that all speaking voices will blend on the same syllable at the same time.

LESSON IX – VOCABULARY DEVELOPMENT

WEARY WORDS:

come	*good*	*walk*	*glad*	*like*	*swell*	*long*
go	*bad*	*think*	*sorry*	*hate*	*lousy*	*short*
scared	*bring*	*dumb*	*fix*	*real*	*give*	*want*
funny	*make*	*mad*	*thing*	*hope*	*take*	*get*

Are these your crutch words? Are you still leaning upon them and a few more like them to express your thoughts? There is nothing wrong with words like these. They are just no longer adequate to express maturing thought with precision, discrimination, and charm. A limited supply of words restricts the activity and growth of the mind.

There are many ways to increase your vocabulary. Reading good books is one of the best, but there are some people who, even though they read a great deal, fail to make use of the enrichment of expression offered them on the printed page. Others grasp at new words and repeat them in sentences without regard to their exact shade of meaning. We must be discriminating in our choice of words. A few good dictionary games will do wonders for your command of your language.

PRACTICE DISCRIMINATION IN WORDS:

Choose just the right word to convey your slightest shade of meaning. Instead of being just *glad* or *sorry*, use the dictionary, or Roget's *Thesaurus,* to find other words that would more precisely describe your feelings. Then find words to complete the following ideas:

Instead of being just smart *or* dumb, *your friend may be—*
You may like him because he is—
Or you may dislike him because he is—

List the weary words we so often modify with *very*, such as *old, funny,* etc. Then find single adjectives to express more precise meanings.

What are SYNONYMS and ANTONYMS? List words and see how many synonyms you can find for each. Find the precise antonyms for words like *lazy, ignorant, benevolent, liberal,* etc.

List words like *glance, silence, condition,* etc. Then list adjectives that describe, or tell what kind of *glance,* etc.

Writing definitions is an excellent aid in vocabulary building. A definition must not contain the word itself or a word closely connected with it, and one should avoid saying *is when* or *is where.* Choose nouns, adjectives, and verbs and try writing good definitions of them.

Perhaps you can think of other good vocabulary-building ideas. The important thing is to apply what you are learning in your own speaking and writing situations.

LESSON X – WORD ROOTS

Knowledge of a few common word roots, or word families, may help you to recognize the meaning of some unfamiliar words. Many of these roots are derived from the Latin language. Since our language is constantly changing, the study could become very complicated. A simple survey, however, may be very helpful.[1]

LATIN ROOTS: Some of the parts of Latin words that have survived as our word roots are given below along with their general

[1] See Margaret S. Ernst, *Words, English Roots and How They Grow* (New York: Alfred A. Knopf and Co., 1950), pp. 61-63, and Ward S. Miller, *Word Wealth* (New York: Henry Holt and Co., 1958), pp. 81-142.

meanings and, in italic type, one word in which the root occurs. You may want to find several related words.

1. aqua—water *aquarium*
2. am—love *amorous*
3. aud—hear *auditory*
4. cant—sing *cantor*
5. carn—flesh *carnivorous*
6. cent—hundred *centennial*
7. corp—body *corporation*
8. crue—cross *crucial*
9. cur—care *curator*
10. dec—ten *decimal*
11. dom—lord *dominion*
12. dur—hard *durable*
13. fac—easy *facility*
14. fide—faith *fidelity*
15. flu—flow *fluent*
16. leg—law or to send *delegate*
17. lic—allow *license*
18. lit—letter *literary*
19. luc—shine *elucidate*
20. long—long *elongate*
21. loq—speak *loquacious*
22. man—hand *manual*
23. med—middle *intermediary*
24. nat—birth *native*
25. nom—name *nominate*
26. prove—prove *disapproval*
27. quad—four *quadrangle*
28. rap—seize *rapacious*
29. son—sound *consonant*
30. ten—hold *tenacious*
31. ven—come *convene*
32. ver—true *veracity*
33. vest—clothing *vestments*
34. viv—life *vivacity*

GREEK ROOTS: From the Greek language we get these word roots:

1. anthropo—man *anthropology*
2. ast—star *astrology*
3. bio—life *biography*
4. chron—time *chronicle*
5. derm—skin *epidermis*
6. gam—marriage *bigamy*
7. gen—race *genealogy*
8. graph—write *autograph*
9. log—word *dialog*
10. meter—measure *barometer*
11. micro—small *microscope*
12. mono—single *monotonous*
13. crat—to rule *aristocracy*
14. path—suffering *antipathy*
15. pet—stone *petrify*
16. phil—love *philanthropy*
17. phobia—fear *claustrophobia*
18. soph—wise *philosopher*
19. tele—far *telescope*
20. theo—a god *theology*

PREFIXES: A prefix is one or more syllables used as the first part of a word to modify its meaning. A study of a few of the most common prefixes may help you to gain the meaning of an unfamiliar word.

1. a—not *atheism*
2. amb or emp—on both sides *ambassador*
3. ante—before *antecedent*
4. anti—against *antidote*
5. auto—self *autograph*
6. bi—two *bilingual*
7. bene—well *benediction*
8. circum—around *circumnavigate*
9. co—together *cooperation*
10. con—against *contradict*
11. demi—half *demigod*
12. dis—not *displease*
13. homo—same *homonym*
14. in—not *inactive*
15. intra—with *intramural*
16. juxta—next to *juxtaposition*
17. mal—bad *malady*
18. mis—wrong *misnomer*
19. multi—many *multimillionaire*
20. non—not *nondescript*
21. per—through or by *perennial*
22. peri—around *perimeter*
23. poly—many *polygamy*
24. post—after *postgraduate*
25. pre—before *presentiment*
26. preter—beyond *preternatural*
27. retro—backward or behind *retrospect*
28. semi—half *semi-formal*
29. sym—together with *sympathy*
30. sub—under or below *subconscious*
31. super—above or over *supercilious*
32. trans—across *transfusion*
33. tri—three *triangle*
34. un—one *unilateral*

SUFFIXES: The syllables added after the word roots are suffixes. For each suffix in the list below:

(1) See how many root words you can list to which the suffix can be added.

(2) Divide the words into the four classes; nouns, verbs, adjectives, and adverbs.

acy	ent	ish	most
ade	er	ist	ness
age	ese	ite	ous
al	ess	ive	ship
an	est	ize	some
ance	ful	le	ster
ant	fy	less	tacle
ate	hood	let	ure
ble	ing	ly	ward
cle	ion	ment	y

13 *Pattern Practice Exercises*

The directions and the exercises given below are worded as the teacher might present them to high-school students.

LESSON I – DRILL WITH THOUGHT

DIRECTIONS:

(1) Repeat the following expressions aloud adding words to complete each thought. If possible, record this exercise on tape and listen to the play-back, or work in pairs and listen to each other. Check any of the sentences that do not sound like your usual pattern of expression. Later, write the sentence the way you would most naturally express the same thought. Study your expression. Unless it is equally acceptable in the area where you now live, practice the new pattern until you have made it your own.

1. *I did ____.*
2. *I didn't have any ____.*
3. *I brought my ____.*
4. *I have written a ____.*
5. *I saw the picture in ____.*
6. *It doesn't ____.*
7. *He ran down ____.*
8. *You were in ____.*
9. *They have come to ____.*
10. *She said she ____.*
11. *He leaves every day at ____.*
12. *Today he left at ____.*
13. *Have you eaten your ____?*
14. *He has a ____.*
15. *We know that he ____.*
16. *They say that ____.*
17. *Yes, it does make ____.*
18. *He loves to go to ____.*
19. *Yes, you are ____.*
20. *They hit him on ____.*
21. *The boy has a ____.*
22. *That means that ____.*
23. *They wear ____.*
24. *They're going to ____*

25. We weren't going to ——.
26. Aren't they going to ——?
27. You're late for ——.
28. That makes it ——.
29. What do they have to ——?
30. He took my ——.
31. I have a new ——.
32. They have no ——.
33. They haven't any ——.
34. They don't want ——.
35. They write ——.
36. I play football and ——.
37. She cried all ——.
38. She cries too ——.
39. I work at ——.
40. Are there any in ——?

(2) How does "When in Rome, do as the Romans do" apply to speech? We like to be fashionable in dress. Why not be fashionable in speech as well?

Complete the thought as you read the following over tape or work in pairs:

1. They pay my ——.
2. I clean —— every day.
3. We love ——.
4. We have enough ——.
5. I like ——.
6. They like to ——.
7. He was graduated last ——.
8. I cleaned the —— yesterday.
9. Yesterday I took ——.
10. He took her ——.
11. He kept ——.
12. Last night I won a ——.
13. He gave me two ——.
14. I want you to ——.
15. He asked if I would ——.
16. She asked if they could ——.
17. If I'd known, I'd have ——.
18. She's very ——.
19. He's absent from ——.
20. You're going to ——.
21. Who's there in the ——?
22. They're both ——.
23. What's your highest ——?
24. What do you ——?
25. You're coming, aren't ——?
26. Now you're ——.
27. He's twenty ——.
28. He took her to ——.
29. She helped her ——.
30. You can't help ——.
31. Throw the ball to ——.
32. Thanks a ——.
33. Two men are ——.
34. Those people are ——.
35. Sometimes I ——.
36. How many women are ——?

37. *That's mine, and this is ____.*
38. *I paid for two ____.*
39. *A lot of people are ____.*
40. *It's fifty cents for ____.*

(3) Completing the thought as you read the following exercises aloud keeps your mind on what you are saying. Check for further practice the ones which are not a part of your regular speech patterns.

1. *It costs five cents to ____.*
2. *There wasn't any use in ____.*
3. *Unless you go, I ____.*
4. *That's his, ____.*
5. *You aren't listening to ____.*
6. *She lives with her ____.*
7. *There were two sisters who ____.*
8. *There are a lot of ____.*
9. *I'm going to ____.*
10. *Her children are ____.*
11. *Her hair is too ____.*
12. *It's a nice day, isn't ____?*
13. *That's my pen on ____.*
14. *That is ____!*
15. *She is home, I ____.*
16. *He isn't in ____.*
17. *He's well and ____*
18. *It's taken, but that seat ____.*
19. *Since I went, I ____.*
20. *Since she's not here, she ____.*
21. *I don't have any ____.*
22. *I haven't any ____.*
23. *Don't say anything to ____.*
24. *I don't know any ____.*
25. *It's not anything you'd ____.*
26. *You and I are going ____.*
27. *She and I went ____.*
28. *Nothing is happening to ____.*
29. *I'm not going that ____.*
30. *I'm not going to do ____.*
31. *You're not going ____.*
32. *Really I'm not ____.*
33. *It isn't ____.*
34. *You have ____.*
35. *You are my ____.*
36. *You're wrong about ____.*
37. *I saw him last ____.*
38. *He ate his ____.*
39. *Anything I said I ____.*
40. *My brother took ____.*

(4) An educated person's basic speech pattern should serve him well wherever he may travel in this country; and in foreign countries, it should represent good American speech. Follow the directions for the previous exercises.

1. *My sister went* ——.
2. *Let's go* ——.
3. *That book is* ——.
4. *This boy is* ——.
5. *He doesn't* ——.
6. *Set the plate on* ——.
7. *They've been* ——.
8. *I'm not* ——.
9. *Yes, I am* ——.
10. *I thought I knew your* ——.
11. *I know I've seen* ——.
12. *Are you listening to* ——.
13. *We're going to* ——.
14. *He doesn't like* ——.
15. *You make me* ——.
16. *She is not* ——.
17. *I mean it. I'm not* ——.
18. *She doesn't want* ——.
19. *What are you talking* ——?
20. *Why do you say* ——?
21. *Why, surely I'll* ——.
22. *Certainly he'll* ——.
23. *I certainly am not* ——.
24. *Surely you* ——.
25. *You had better* ——.
26. *You should* ——.
27. *I am finished with* ——.
28. *Yes, I'll* ——.
29. *Yes, he is* ——.
30. *Listen to that* ——.
31. *Would you like to dance this* ——?
32. *Do you care to* ——?
33. *Shall we* ——?
34. *Would you like to go to the* ——?
35. *He thinks he's* ——.
36. *It makes no difference to* ——.
37. *Yes, I would like to* ——.
38. *Is it true that* ——?
39. *Is that the* ——?
40. *I understand what* ——.
41. *I'll see you* ——.
42. *What kind of* ——?
43. *He could have been* ——.
44. *He might have taken* ——.
45. *The second Tuesday in January is* ——.
46. *What's happening* ——?
47. *Is it up there or down* ——?
48. *Who's that* ——?
49. *You are wrong, but they are* ——.
50. *You were there when* ——.
51. *Were you there after* ——?
52. *I saw him at the* ——.
53. *He saw me when I* ——.
54. *You fellows were* ——.
55. *We were going* ——.
56. *We were taking a* ——.
57. *Were we later than* ——?
58. *It doesn't seem* ——.
59. *May I please have* ——?
60. *Excuse me, but* ——.

LESSON II — TONGUE TWISTERS

EXERCISE:

(1) For lazy lips and sluggish tongue, recite each of these tough tongue twisters three times in rapid succession.

1. A big black bug bit a big black bear, made a big black bear bleed.
2. Fanny Finch fried five floundering fish for Francis Fowler's father.
3. What whim led "Whitey" White to whittle, whistle, whisper, and whimper near the wharf where a whale might wheel and whirl?
4. Thomas Tatterfoot took taut twine to tie ten twigs to two tall trees.
5. The path of wrath may lead to death for both.
6. Slippery sleds slide smoothly down the sluiceway.
7. Amidst the mists and coldest frosts
With barest wrists and stoutest boasts
He thrusts his fists against the posts
And still insists he sees the ghosts.
8. During the night he was doing his homework down in the dining room.
9. She sells sea shells by the seashore.
10. The seething sea ceaseth, and thus the seething sea recedeth.
11. Does this shop stock short socks with spots?
12. A thatcher of Thatchwood went to Thatchet a-thatching;
Did a thatcher of Thatchwood go to Thatchet a-thatching?
If a thatcher of Thatchwood went to Thatchet a-thatching,
Where's that thatching the thatcher of Thatchwood has thatched?
13. Theophilus Thistle, the thistle sifter, sifted a sieve of unsifted thistles.
If Theophilus Thistle, the thistle sifter, sifted a sieve of unsifted thistles,
Where is the sieve of unsifted thistles Theophilus Thistle, the thistle sifter, sifted?

14. Around the rugged rock the ragged rascal ran.
15. Three gray geese in the green grass grazing; gray were the geese, and green was the grazing.
16. The old scold sold the school a coal scuttle.
17. The rain fell on the plain in Spain.
18. How many people were there? There were four men, five women, and nine children.
19. He held the icicle high and then let it drop right beside the frightened child.
20. He's a man of might,
    Too fat to fight.
    Yes, a rat, that's right!
    Waving hat on high,
    And not batting an eye
    As he shouts his lie
    While the people cry.
21. Trace the tree on a stencil with pencil. Then we'll trim them with tinsel.
22. I'd rather have fingers than toes;
    I'd rather have ears than a nose;
    And as for my hair
    I'm glad it's all there,
    I'll be awfully sad when it goes.

—GELETT BURGESS

(2) Choose the sound in which you need most practice. Try making up your own practice drills and using them.

LESSON III — AVOIDING SUBSTITUTIONS

SUBSTITUTION OF *D*, *T*, OR *F* FOR THE *TH* SOUND:

EXERCISE:

(1) Repeat the following pairs of words: Be careful not to substitute the sound of *d*, *t*, or *f* for *th*.

1. *tank–thank*
2. *tankful–thankful*
3. *tong–thong*
4. *Tum–thumb*
5. *bird–third*
6. *rat–wrath*
7. *loaf–loathe*
8. *deaf–death*
9. *ate–eighth*
10. *bat–bath*
11. *bate–bathe*
12. *wharf–North*
13. *string–strength*
14. *orphan–Northeastern*
15. *whistle–thistle*
16. *tin–thin*
17. *Waldorf–forth*
18. *ting–thing*
19. *tease–thesis*
20. *breeze–these*
21. *'tis–this*
22. *fetter–feather*
23. *enter–either*
24. *coating–clothing*
25. *beat–breathe*
26. *wit–with*
27. *skate–scathe*
28. *clawed–cloth*
29. *clover–clothe*
30. *bet–Beth*

(2) Repeat these sentences:

1. *This thing was thrown in the thicket.*
2. *The deaf orphan asked what was thrown with it.*
3. *Three things went with it: feathers, cloth, and thatch.*
4. *I'm thankful for the third.*
5. *Either both shall go with you or neither.*
6. *They both were too near death with little strength to breathe.*
7. *This thin clothing seems just feather weight in the North.*
8. *They are seething with wrath and loathing.*

SUBSTITUTION OF *OWN* FOR *ON*:

Strongly stressed *o* as in *mote* plus *oo* as in *cool* should not be substituted for *a* as in *calm.*

EXERCISE:

(1) Do you say *Come own* for *Come on*? Clear up this confusion by repeating the following combinations of words:

1. *soak–sot*
2. *tote–tot*
3. *own–on*
4. *boat–box*
5. *coat–cot*
6. *hope–hop*
7. *goat–got*
8. *beaux–bop*
9. *slow–slop*
10. *crow–crop*
11. *cloak–clock*
12. *foe–fop*
13. *fro–frock*
14. *Stroh–strop*
15. *row–rock*
16. *doe–dock*
17. *pole–pock*
18. *toe–top*
19. *woe–wad*
20. *sow–sod*

(2) Repeat these sentences:

1. *Once upon a time I got to bop on a rock-'n'-roll show.*
2. *He ran on and on to the pond.*
3. *The little tot hopped onto the cot.*
4. *Come on, now. I'm waiting. Come on!*
5. *I'll go on home. You'll come on later.*

LESSON IV – GAINING CLEARNESS

SUBSTITUTING *PINNEY* FOR *PENNY*

Your meaning will not be clear if you confuse the vowels in such words as *pin* and *pen*. The following words have the same vowel sound as the word for a writing tool, *pen*. They should not have the vowel sound in *pin*:

1. *gentlemen*
2. *many*
3. *when*
4. *any*
5. *anybody*
6. *anyone*
7. *general*
8. *condemned*
9. *again*
10. *anything*
11. *went*
12. *rent*
13. *sensible*
14. *amend*
15. *contend*
16. *fence*
17. *spent*
18. *plenty*
19. *tense*
20. *extend*
21. *offend*
22. *adventure*
23. *twenty*
24. *enemy*

EXERCISE: Practice repeating the following pairs of words.

1. *tin–ten*
2. *mint–meant*
3. *him–hem*
4. *bin–Ben*
5. *Jim–gem*
6. *bit–bet*
7. *tint–tent*
8. *sinned–send*
9. *hit–get*

SLURRING OR OMITTING SYLLABLES

All syllables of the following words should be pronounced clearly. Do not omit medial syllables or parts of syllables. For instance, say " government," not " gov'munt."

EXERCISE: Practice by repeating these words:

1. pronunciation	*5. serious*	*9. Mississippi*	*13. attention*
2. enunciation	*6. miserable*	*10. borrowed*	*14. exactly*
3. association	*7. Alabama*	*11. recognize*	*15. positive*
4. quarrelled	*8. Louisiana*	*12. realize*	*16. carried*

MEDIAL *R* [*r*]

EXERCISE: Pronounce these words without omitting the medial sound made by the letter *r*.

1. very	*5. worry*	*9. Harry*	*13. tarry*
2. marry	*6. ferry*	*10. berry*	*14. surrey*
3. hurry	*7. Jerry*	*11. furry*	*15. environment*
4. carry	*8. Larry*	*12. flurry*	*16. occurrence*

FALSE, LINKING *R*

EXERCISE:

Pronounce these words without adding a false, linking *r* sound:

1. doing his homework	*6. following*
2. the idea of it!	*7. Florida and Louisiana*
3. raw oysters	*8. Georgia and Florida*
4. law and order	*9. hollowing*
5. soda and malted	

THREE VOWELS FOR ONE

Do you use three vowel sounds where one is more effective? Do you lower your jaw to say " gaoulden " for " golden " and " La-ourd " for " Lord "? If so, your meaning may not be clear, as you can hear by repeating the following pairs of words.

EXERCISE:

(1) Give just one separate clear vowel sound to each of the following:

1. *Lord—lard*
2. *born—barn*
3. *store—star*
4. *form—farm*
5. *cord—card*
6. *chore—char*
7. *port—part*
8. *adorn—darn*
9. *tort—tart*
10. *pored—pard*
11. *bore—bar*
12. *corpse—carps*
13. *deport—depart*
14. *torn—tarn*
15. *former—farmer*
16. *stork—stark*
17. *horde—hard*
18. *rolled—rallied*
19. *morn—marne*
20. *Norton—Martin*
21. *sport—spark*
22. *gore—gar*

(2) Repeat these sentences:

1. *This morning the stork came to the farm and left a little form.*
2. *The bold store clerk scalded his forearm with the hot lard.*
3. *He rolled the assortment of corn, celery hearts, corks, and lard together and tied them with a cord.*
4. *Mr. Norton retorted that he had been deported.*
5. *That morn the store was adorned with torn paper stars and confetti.*

(3) Make up similar exercises to correct other deviations from acceptable speech. Help yourself to a good life through good speech.

APPENDIX A

The Questionnaire

SPEECH IMPROVEMENT

A KEY TO BETTER UNDERSTANDING

FORD FOUNDATION FELLOWSHIP PROGRAM

THE FUND FOR THE ADVANCEMENT OF EDUCATION

The following instrument, designed for both upper level high school students and adults, is for the purpose, in general, of helping people to get along better together. More specifically, it is to help meet a language problem in a Midwestern city high school. Many other schools may have a similar problem. Your time spent in marking the answers will be a fine contribution to this project. You need not sign your name.

DIRECTIONS: FIRST READ THE QUESTION AND ALL POSSIBLE CHOICES GIVEN FOR THE ANSWER. THEN CHECK (√) YOUR CORRECT CHOICE, OR FILL IN THE BLANKS. (KINDLY DISREGARD THE SYSTEM OF NUMBERS, WHICH WILL BE USED IN TABULATING RESULTS.)

Individual Project of

Ruth I. Golden, 40 Colorado Avenue, Highland Park 3, Michigan

November 1, 1955

PERSONAL INFORMATION

Date ____________

Code No. ____________

1) 2) 3) 4)

(5) CHECK: Are you a 1) _____ Student
2) _____ Adult
3) _____ Male
4) _____ Female

FILL IN THE BLANKS BELOW. DISREGARD CODE NO.

(6) If student, name your school: ______________. Code No. __

(7) If adult, give your occupation: ______________. Code No. __

(8) Occupation of father or guardian, if living (write *Not Employed* if that is the case):

______________. Code No. __

(9) Occupation of mother or guardian, if living (write *Not Employed* if that is the case):

______________. Code No. __

(10) Give the city (or county) and state where you
(11) were born: ______________________. Code No. __

(12) Where did you start school? Give the city (or
(13) county) and state: ______________________ Code No. __

(14) Name one other state, if any, in which you,
(15) your parents, or grandparents have lived:

______________________. Code No. __

(16) Name the last school you attended: __________.
Check the kind of school it was:

1) _____ Elementary
2) _____ Intermediate or Junior High School
3) _____ High School
4) _____ College
5) _____ University

(17) Where was this last school located?

____

(18) City State

(19) What is the highest grade you have completed?

(20). (Count the first year of college as grade 13.) ___ Code No. ___

(21) What is the highest degree you hold, if any?

CHECK: 1) ____ B. A. or B. S.
2) ____ M. A. or M. S.
3) ____ Ph. D.
4) ____ LL. B.
5) ____ LL. D.
6) ____ M. D.
7) ____ DDS.
8) ____ D. O.
9) ____ D. D.
10) ____ Other

(22) By whom were you reared during your first five years when your speech pattern was being formed?

1) ____ Mother
2) ____ Grandmother
3) ____ Aunt
4) ____ Sister
5) ____ Some other person or persons

(23) What is the highest school level completed by the person who reared you?

1) ____ Grades 1 or 2
2) ____ Grades 3 or 4
3) ____ Grades 5 or 6
4) ____ Grades 7 or 8
5) ____ Grades 9 or 10
6) ____ Grades 11 or 12
7) ____ 1 or 2 years of college
8) ____ 3 or 4 years of colege
9) ____ 5 or more years of college

(24) What is the highest school level completed by your father or the man closest to you during your first five years?

1) ____ Grades 1 or 2
2) ____ Grades 3 or 4
3) ____ Grades 5 or 6
4) ____ Grades 7 or 8

5) ____ Grades 9 or 10
6) ____ Grades 11 or 12
7) ____ 1 or 2 years of college
8) ____ 3 or 4 years of college
9) ____ 5 or more years of college

(25) With whom did you live during your first five years?

1) ____ Both parents
2) ____ Mother alone
3) ____ Father alone
4) ____ Father and stepmother
5) ____ Mother and stepfather
6) ____ Institution
7) ____ Grandparents
8) ____ Guardians
9) ____ Other relatives

(26) Check which of the following are brought regularly into your home for you to read if you wish: (You may check as many as five, or you may leave all blank if you don't have any of them.)

1) ____ A daily newspaper
2) ____ A weekly news magazine
3) ____ A hobby or fiction magazine
4) ____ A literary magazine
5) ____ A humor magazine
6) ____ Some other paper or magazine

(27) Check the approximate number of books you have in your home library.

1) ____ 0-9
2) ____ 10-19
3) ____ 20-29
4) ____ 30-39
5) ____ 40-49
6) ____ 50 or more

(28) How often do you and your family attend religious services?

1) ____ Never
2) ____ Once a year
3) ____ Three or four times a year

4) _____ Six or eight times a year
5) _____ Once a month
6) _____ Twice a month
7) _____ Usually once a week
8) _____ Usually twice a week
9) _____ Usually more often than twice a week

(29) Have you ever talked to a stranger on the telephone and by his way of speaking been able to picture him as belonging to a particular racial or nationality group?

1) _____ Yes
2) _____ No

In talking to a stranger on the telephone, do you sometimes form conclusions as to his "learning"?

4) _____ Yes
5) _____ No

Do you think these conclusions could sometimes be wrong?

7) _____ Yes
8) _____ No

EXPRESSIONS

BELOW IS A LIST OF EXPRESSIONS FREQUENTLY USED BY SOME PEOPLE. CHECK:

COLUMN I — EACH OF THE EXPRESSIONS WHICH YOU MAY HEAR EVERY DAY.

COLUMN II — EACH OF THE EXPRESSIONS WHICH YOU MAY EVER HAVE HEARD A HIGH SCHOOL GRADUATE USE.

COLUMN III — EACH OF THE EXPRESSIONS WHICH YOU YOURSELF MAY EVER USE.

FOR EACH EXPRESSION, YOU MAY CHECK ONE, TWO OR ALL THREE COLUMNS. LEAVE UNCHECKED ONLY THOSE EXPRESSIONS WHICH SOUND UNFAMILIAR OR UNCOMMON TO YOU.

EXAMPLE: 1) _____ 2) _____ 3) _____ *I done it.*

IF YOU RECOGNIZE *I done it* AS BEING A VERY FAMILIAR EXPRESSION TO YOU, ONE WHICH YOU MIGHT HEAR EVERY DAY, YOU WOULD CHECK 1) __√__.

IF YOU HAVE EVER HEARD A HIGH SCHOOL GRADUATE USE THE EXPRESSION, *I done it,* ALSO CHECK 2) __√__.

IF YOU THINK YOU YOURSELF MAY EVER USE THAT EXPRESSION, ALSO CHECK 3) __√__.

THEN THE EXAMPLE WOULD LOOK LIKE THIS:

1) __√__ 2) __√__ 3) __√__ *I done it.*

IF YOU HEAR *I done it* OFTEN AND HAVE HEARD A HIGH SCHOOL GRADUATE USE IT, BUT YOU ARE SURE YOU YOURSELF WOULD NEVER SAY IT EVEN WHEN TALKING TO FAMILY AND FRIENDS, THE EXAMPLE WOULD LOOK LIKE THIS:

1) __√__ 2) __√__ 3) ____ *I done it.*

DISREGARD THE NUMBERING SYSTEM. CHECK THE COLUMNS.

	COL. I HEAR OFTEN	COL. II GRAD. USES	COL. III YOU USE	
(30)	1) ____	2) ____	3) ____	I done it.
	5) ____	6) ____	7) ____	Didn't have nothin'.
	9) ____	0) ____	X) ____	I brung my book.
(31)	1) ____	2) ____	3) ____	I have wrote.
	5) ____	6) ____	7) ____	I seen the pi'ture.
	9) ____	0) ____	X) ____	It don't.
(32)	1) ____	2) ____	3) ____	I sung it.
	5) ____	6) ____	7) ____	He run home.
	9) ____	0) ____	X) ____	You was there.
(33)	1) ____	2) ____	3) ____	They have came.
	5) ____	6) ____	7) ____	Heesa no here.
	9) ____	0) ____	X) ____	She say–
(34)	1) ____	2) ____	3) ____	He leave.
	5) ____	6) ____	7) ____	Has you eat?
	9) ____	0) ____	X) ____	He have a–
(35)	1) ____	2) ____	3) ____	We all knows that, man!
	5) ____	6) ____	7) ____	They says–
	9) ____	0) ____	X) ____	Yes, it do!

	COL. I HEAR OFTEN	COL. II GRAD. USES	COL. III YOU USE	
(36)	1) ____	2) ____	3) ____	He love to go.
	5) ____	6) ____	7) ____	He go there.
	9) ____	0) ____	X) ____	Yes, you is!
(37)	1) ____	2) ____	3) ____	They hits him.
	5) ____	6) ____	7) ____	The boy have a dog.
	9) ____	0) ____	X) ____	That mean–
(38)	1) ____	2) ____	3) ____	They's goin'.
	5) ____	6) ____	7) ____	They wears–
	9) ____	0) ____	X) ____	It sho' have.
(39)	1) ____	2) ____	3) ____	Isn't they?
	5) ____	6) ____	7) ____	You's late.
	9) ____	0) ____	X) ____	That make it nice.
(40)	1) ____	2) ____	3) ____	What all they has to do?
	5) ____	6) ____	7) ____	He take mah pahncil.
	9) ____	0) ____	X) ____	I gots me a new hat.
(41)	1) ____	2) ____	3) ____	They has no more.
	5) ____	6) ____	7) ____	They doesn't want to.
	9) ____	0) ____	X) ____	They writes letters.
(42)	1) ____	2) ____	3) ____	I plays golf.
	5) ____	6) ____	7) ____	She cry all night.
	9) ____	0) ____	X) ____	I works hard.
(43)	1) ____	2) ____	3) ____	Like so many has done.
	5) ____	6) ____	7) ____	They pays my rent.
	9) ____	0) ____	X) ____	I cleans good.
(44)	1) ____	2) ____	3) ____	We loves it.
	5) ____	6) ____	7) ____	We has enough.
	9) ____	0) ____	X) ____	I likes things nice.
(45)	1) ____	2) ____	3) ____	They likes to go.
	5) ____	6) ____	7) ____	He graduate last June.
	9) ____	0) ____	X) ____	I clean house yesterday.
(46)	1) ____	2) ____	3) ____	Yesterday I take–
	5) ____	6) ____	7) ____	He taken her home.
	9) ____	0) ____	X) ____	He keep it.

	COL. I HEAR OFTEN	COL. II GRAD. USES	COL. III YOU USE	
(47)	1) ____	2) ____	3) ____	Last night I win it.
	5) ____	6) ____	7) ____	He give me two.
	9) ____	0) ____	X) ____	I want for you to–
(48)	1) ____	2) ____	3) ____	He asked would I go.
	5) ____	6) ____	7) ____	Did I know, I'd a went.
	9) ____	0) ____	X) ____	She real happy.
(49)	1) ____	2) ____	3) ____	He absent.
	5) ____	6) ____	7) ____	You goin', hear?
	9) ____	0) ____	X) ____	Who dere?
(50)	1) ____	2) ____	3) ____	They bofe gone.
	5) ____	6) ____	7) ____	What yo' ha'a school?
	9) ____	0) ____	X) ____	What yo' mean, gal?
(51)	1) ____	2) ____	3) ____	You comin', ain't you?
	5) ____	6) ____	7) ____	Now you talkin'.
	9) ____	0) ____	X) ____	He twenty-one.
(52)	1) ____	2) ____	3) ____	He carry her to church.
	5) ____	6) ____	7) ____	She hope him.
	9) ____	0) ____	X) ____	You can't hope her.
(53)	1) ____	2) ____	3) ____	Chunk the ball.
	5) ____	6) ____	7) ____	Doin' the day.
	9) ____	0) ____	X) ____	Thanks a lots.
(54)	1) ____	2) ____	3) ____	Two mens–
	5) ____	6) ____	7) ____	Those peoples–
	9) ____	0) ____	X) ____	Sometime I do.
(55)	1) ____	2) ____	3) ____	How many womens there?
	5) ____	6) ____	7) ____	That's mines.
	9) ____	0) ____	X) ____	I pay for twenty year.
(56)	1) ____	2) ____	3) ____	A lots of peoples–
	5) ____	6) ____	7) ____	It's fifty cent.
	9) ____	0) ____	X) ____	It cost fa've cent.
(57)	1) ____	2) ____	3) ____	'Twan't no use.
	5) ____	6) ____	7) ____	Unlessen–
	9) ____	0) ____	X) ____	That's his'n, honey chile!

	COL. I HEAR OFTEN	COL. II GRAD. USES	COL. III YOU USE	
(58)	1) ____	2) ____	3) ____	Y'all ain't listenin'.
	5) ____	6) ____	7) ____	She stays by her auntie's.
	9) ____	0) ____	X) ____	It's a two sisters–
(59)	1) ____	2) ____	3) ____	They's a lots a–
	5) ____	6) ____	7) ____	I's fixin' to–
	9) ____	0) ____	X) ____	Chillun all growed–
(60)	1) ____	2) ____	3) ____	Her hair are too long.
	5) ____	6) ____	7) ____	Nice day, ain't?
	9) ____	0) ____	X) ____	That be my ink pen.
(61)	1) ____	2) ____	3) ____	That do be nice!
	5) ____	6) ____	7) ____	She be's home.
	9) ____	0) ____	X) ____	He don't be here.
(62)	1) ____	2) ____	3) ____	He be's well.
	5) ____	6) ____	7) ____	It be taken.
	9) ____	0) ____	X) ____	Bein's I went–
(63)	1) ____	2) ____	3) ____	Bein' she's not here–
	5) ____	6) ____	7) ____	You be wrong.
	9) ____	0) ____	X) ____	They be gone.

(64) Do you believe that certain expressions like those you have just read help to identify persons with particular racial or nationality groups?

1) ____ Yes
2) ____ No

Do you believe that people outside of a particular group might think that if a person has "learning," he will use the language teaching he gets in school and through good reading and listening?

4) ____ Yes
5) ____ No

Do you think that people outside of the group might get a wrong idea about a person's "learning" if they hear him use some of these expressions?

7) ____ Yes
8) ____ No

(65) Do you think the use of such expressions could keep a person from being accepted into other social groups?

1) ____ Yes
2) ____ No

Do you think the use of these expressions could keep a person from getting some types of jobs?

4) ____ Yes
5) ____ No

Do you think that some expressions common to a group may sound amusing and even laughable to some people of another group?

7) ____ Yes
8) ____ No

(66) Do you agree that the dignity or standing of a racial or national group is not helped by those whose speech may cause others to laugh at them?

1) ____ Yes
2) ____ No

If certain expressions may give the wrong idea about a person's "learning" and may cause some people to be laughed at, do you think it would help people to get along better together if they made more of an effort to overcome such expressions?

4) ____ Yes
5) ____ No

Most people speak somewhat differently when speaking to family and friends from the way they speak in the classroom or to adults or strangers. Do you?

7) ____ Yes
8) ____ No

(67) How free from grammatical errors is your own speech to family and friends?

1) ____ I always use good speech that is free from grammatical errors.

2) ____ I use some slang expressions, but no grammatical errors.

3) _____ I may use some grammatical errors and slang expressions.
4) _____ I probably use many grammatical errors and slang expressions.
5) _____ I use many of the expressions listed in this questionaire and others like them.

(68) If there is a wide grammatical difference between the speech you know how to use and the speech you do use when talking to your family and friends, can you give any reason why this should be?

1) _____ They wouldn't understand me.
2) _____ They'd think I was better than they.
3) _____ They'd think I didn't belong to the group.
4) _____ They'd think I was putting on airs.
5) _____ I have some other reason.

(69) If you have checked (5), would you care to state the reason here? ________________________________.

(70) Have you ever felt a need or a desire to use better grammar?

1) _____ Yes
2) _____ No

(71) If *yes,* at approximately what age did you begin to feel such a need or a desire?

1) _____ Age 6
2) _____ Age 8
3) _____ Age 10
4) _____ Age 12
5) _____ Age 14
6) _____ Age 16
7) _____ Age 18
8) _____ Age 20
9) _____ Age 22
0) _____ Age 24
X) _____ Age 26 or over

(72) Which of the following do you think helped the most to make you want to improve? You may check as many as five.

1) _____ A book or books
2) _____ A magazine or newspaper article
3) _____ A movie or film strip you saw
4) _____ A play or program you saw

5) ____ A play or program you took part in
6) ____ A radio or television program you saw
7) ____ A radio or television program you took part in
8) ____ Some other speech-making situation
9) ____ An embarrassing moment
0) ____ A new interest
X) ____ A church situation

(73) 1) ____ A job situation
2) ____ A club situation
3) ____ A party situation
4) ____ A teacher
5) ____ A parent
6) ____ A brother or sister
7) ____ A relative
8) ____ An adult you admired
9) ____ A friend of your sex
0) ____ A friend of the opposite sex
X) ____ Some other factor

(74) From your own experience, which of the following methods do you think help the most to improve speech? You may mark as many as five.

1) ____ Corrections by parents or friends
2) ____ Explanations by teachers
3) ____ Corrections by teachers
4) ____ Explanations read from textbooks or workbooks
5) ____ Written exercises (corrected and discussed) in which you choose correct forms
6) ____ Written exercises in which you write sentences using certain forms of grammar
7) ____ Original compositions which you rewrite to correct your errors
8) ____ Writing errors on pocket cards to be carried until the errors are overcome
9) ____ Oral talks with class corrections of errors
0) ____ Oral talks with corrections given by the teacher
X) ____ Oral talks with written corrections by the class and teacher

(75) 1) ____ Oral grammar drills in which you indicate whether a statement is correct or incorrect

2) _____ Oral grammar drills in which you choose correct forms
3) _____ Oral repeating of correct forms
4) _____ Class and individual attention to correcting a few errors at a time
5) _____ Class games for pointing out each other's errors
6) _____ Hearing correct forms spoken at home
7) _____ Hearing correct forms spoken at school
8) _____ Hearing correct forms spoken in movies or on radio and television
9) _____ Hearing correct forms spoken at church, theatre, club, or on the job
0) _____ Hearing correct forms spoken elsewhere
X) Some other method

(76) Have you thought of other expressions used by members of your group that were not included in this questionnaire? If so, list them here:

____

____

____

(77) Do you know of other good ways of correcting language that were not listed? If so, write them here:

____

____

____

(78) Below, name any books, plays, television programs, movies, or film strips which you think are especially good in helping people to get along better together. To show which each is, write B, P, TV, M, or F, after each title

____

____

____

(79) Below, name any books (other than school books), plays, television programs, movies or film strips which you think are especially good in helping people to speak better. Write B, P, TV, M, or F after each title.

____

____

____

APPENDIX B

1: Persons Interviewed

Adams, L. D., Assistant Superintendent, Richmond Public Schools, Richmond, Virginia.

Agren, Raymond, Assistant Principal, Cody High School, Detroit.

Arbaugh, William A., Assistant Principal, Central High School, Detroit.

Bagwell, Paul D., Head of the Department of Communication Skills, Michigan State University, East Lansing, Michigan.

Barrows, Marjorie W., English Editor, Henry Holt and Company, New York.

Beauchamp, Robert, Head of the English Department, Pontiac High School, Pontiac, Michigan.

Beery, John R., Dean of the School of Education, University of Miami, Coral Gables, Florida.

Bergman, Walter G., Director, Department of Instructional Research, Board of Education, Detroit.

Blumenthal, Joseph, Head of the English Department, Mackenzie High School, Detroit.

Boone, David, Teacher of English, Northeastern High School, Detroit.

Carter, Marion, Counselor, Northeastern High School, Detroit.

Cauley, Thomas, Head of the English Department, Denby High School, Detroit.

Cheskie, Sophie V., Head of the Adult Education Department, Highland Park Public Schools, Highland Park, Michigan.

Churchill, Margaret, Teacher, Institute of Language and Linguistics, Georgetown University, Washington, D. C.

Clay, Selena, Counselor, Armstrong High School, Richmond, Virginia.

Cook, Lloyd A., Vice President in Charge of Education and Research, Wayne State University, Detroit.

Cordray, A. T., Director, Improvement Services, Department of

Communication Skills, Michigan State University, East Lansing, Michigan.

Corenman, Herman, National Labor Relations Board, Detroit.

Corey, Stephen, Horace Mann Lincoln Institute of School Experimentation, Columbia University, New York.

Courtis, Stuart A., Professor Emeritus of Education, University of Michigan, Ann Arbor, Michigan.

Crary, Ryland W., N. E. A. Coordinator for the Fund for the Advancement of Education, National Education Association, Washington, D. C.

Dancy, John C., Executive Director, The Urban League, Detroit.

Daugherty, Mildred, English Teacher and former Ford Fellow, Louisville, Kentucky.

Davis, Allison, Department of Education and Research, University of Chicago, Chicago.

Delbridge, Helen, Assistant Principal, Cooley High School, Detroit.

Donovan, Bernard E., Assistant Superintendent of Schools, Board of Education of the City of New York, Brooklyn, New York.

Dresher, Richard, Department of Guidance and Placement, Board of Education, Detroit.

Eddy, Henry, Principal of Northeastern High School, Detroit,

Elson, Milton, Editor, the Oxford Book Company, New York.

Fein, Carl, Executive Secretary, Alumni Association, University of Miami, Coral Gables, Florida.

Fisher, Granville, Chairman of the Department of Psychology, University of Miami, Coral Gables, Florida.

Ford, Elverton, Commercial Teacher, Northeastern High School, Detroit.

Fries, Robert, Head of the English Department, Osborn High School, Detroit.

Galante, Ferdinand, Head of the English Department, Miller High School, Detroit.

Gary, Nancy, Head of the English Department, Thomas Jefferson High School, Richmond, Virginia.

Gholson, G. James, Principal, Fairmont Heights High School, Prince George's County, Maryland.

Golden, David L., Associate Municipal Judge, Highland Park Municipal Court, Highland Park, Michigan.

Graves, Isaac, DDS., Detroit.

Graves, Olga, Hampton University graduate, Detroit.

Green, Marvin, English Teacher, Northern High School, Detroit.

Haelterman, Wallace, Acting Head, Language Department, Northeastern High School, Detroit.

Hale, Edna, Speech Teacher, Armstrong High School, Richmond, Virginia.

Hallock, George, Psychologist, Highland Park Public Schools, Highland Park, Michigan.

Hancock, C. C., Principal, Thomas Jefferson High School, Richmond, Virginia.

Hanlon, Helen, Supervisor, Language Education, Detroit Public Schools, Detroit.

Harrell, William, Principal, Oglethorpe High School, Oglethorpe, Georgia.

Hatscher, Lorraine, Teacher of English and former Ford Fellow, Niles Township High School, Skokie, Illinois.

Harrison, Harold, Assistant Principal, Miller High School, Detroit.

Henderson, Allen, Teacher of Speech, Miller High School, Detroit.

Hoffman, Charles, Head of the Division of Speech, District of Columbia Teachers College, Washington, D. C.

Horsman, Gwen, Reading Consultant, Detroit Public Schools, Detroit.

Isenberg, Robert, Assistant Director, NEA Division of Rural Service, National Education Association, Washington, D. C.

Jackson, Harvey, Counselor, Highland Park High School, Highland Park, Michigan.

Jacobson, Arvid W., Director, Computation Laboratory, Wayne State University, Detroit.

Jay, Edith, Department of Education and Research, Wayne State University, Detroit.

Johnson, Arthur L., Executive Secretary of the NAACP, Detroit.

Kamins, Molly, Teacher of English, Hyde Park High School, Chicago.

Kennedy, Jessie, Counselor, Central High School, Detroit.

Kopp, George, Head of the Speech Department, Wayne State University, Detroit.

Kornegay, Francis A., Director of Vocational Services Department, the Urban League, Detroit.

Kornhauser, Beatrice, Head of the English Department, Hyde Park High School, Chicago.

Kriewitz, Helen, Adjustment Service Department, Hyde Park High School, Chicago.

Kwit, Morris, Head of the English Department, High School of Commerce, New York.

LaBrant, Lou, School of Education, University of Kansas City, Kansas City, Missouri.

Lado, Robert, English Language Institute, University of Michigan, Ann Arbor, Michigan.

Lane, Ralph H., Department of English, District of Columbia Teachers College, Washington, D. C.

Lloyd, Donald J., Department of English, Wayne State University, Detroit.

Lyons, Hope, Dean of Students, District of Columbia Teachers College, Washington, D. C.

Mahoney, Charles H., Great Lakes Mutual Life Insurance Co., and former delegate to the United Nations, Detroit.

Margolis, H. R., Principal, Goodrich Elementary School, Chicago.

Marshall, Ernest T., Senior Administrative Assistant, Guidance and Placement Department, Board of Education, Detroit.

Mathews, W. Mason, President of the Board of Education, Highland Park Public Schools, Highland Park, Michigan.

McCormick, James P., Department of English, Wayne State University, Detroit.

McGrath, A. L., Assistant Superintendent of Schools, Board of Education, Detroit.

Merritt, William, Principal, Miller High School, Detroit.

Mudge, Merrill, Audio Visual Department, Detroit Public Schools, Detroit.

Murray, Donald, Principal, Northern High School, Detroit.

Northcott, Walter, Head of the English Department, Cody High School, Detroit.

Onica, Paul, Teacher of English, Northeastern High School, Detroit.

Pagel, Barnhard, Assistant Director, Division of Research, Board of Education, Detroit.

Payne, Mary W., Head of the English Department, Armstrong High School, Richmond, Virginia.

Perry, Dorothy, Supervisor of Elementary Education, Detroit Public Schools, Detroit.

Peterson, George, Jr., Principal, Armstrong High School, Richmond, Virginia.

Prince, Dorothy, Teacher of Speech, Audio-Visual Center, Agriculture and Technical College, Greensboro, North Carolina.

Provin, Harry H., Director of Alumni Affairs, University of Miami, Coral Gables, Florida.

Puckett, Roy C., Assistant Principal, Thomas Jefferson High School, Richmond, Virginia.

Rasschaert, William M., Department of Instructional Research, Board of Education, Detroit.

Rea, Wesley, Assistant Principal, Northeastern High School, Detroit.

Reitz, William, Department of Education and Research, Wayne State University, Detroit.

Repeta, Genevieve, Teacher of Commercial Subjects, Northeastern High School, Detroit.

Roberts, Marie D., Counselor, Booker T. Washington High School, Miami, Florida.

Robinson, Bertha M., Principal, Central High School, Detroit.

Robinson, Remus, M. D., Member, Board of Education, Detroit Public Schools, Detroit.

Roland, Charles P., Audio-Visual Coordinator, LeMoyne College, Memphis, Tennessee.

Ryan, Robert, Audio-Visual Technician, Northeastern High School, Detroit.

Scott, Sarah, Coordinator of Language Arts, Booker T. Washington High School, Miami, Florida.

Smith, Helen K., Reading Specialist, Niles Township High School, Skokie, Illinois.

Smith, Jeanne G., Head of the English Department, Julia Richman High School, New York.

Smith, Max, Superintendent of Schools, Highland Park, Michigan.

Smith, Sue, Book Review Specialist, Highland Park, Michigan.

Staton, Margaret, Audio-Visual Service, Board of Education, Detroit.

Stratton, Madeline, Teacher of English, A. O. Sexton Elementary School, Chicago.

Swann, F. S., Assistant Principal, Armstrong High School, Richmond, Virginia.

Tharp, Charles Doren, Dean of Faculties, University of Miami, Coral Gables, Florida.

Thompson, Max, Superintendent of Schools, Van Dyke, Michigan.

Tillman, Nathaniel P., Head of the Department of English, Atlanta University and Morehouse College, Atlanta, Georgia.

Triezenberg, George, Assistant Principal, Hyde Park High School, Chicago.

Turner, Edward M., President of the NAACP, Detroit.

Wachner, Clarence, Director of Language Education, Detroit Public Schools, Detroit.

Wallace, Grace, Head of the Department of English, Highland Park High School, Highland Park, Michigan.

Warfel, Harry R., Department of English, University of Florida, Gainesville, Florida.

Watt, Junetta, Guidance and Placement Department, Board of Education, Detroit.

Weiner, Lawrence, Manager, Computation Laboratory, Wayne State University, Detroit.

Whitmer, Floyd, Head of the Language Department, Northern High School, Detroit.

Wight, William S., Associate Professor of English, University of Miami, Coral Gables, Florida.

Williams, Charles, Principal, Booker T. Washington High School, Miami, Florida.

Wimer, Frances, English Teacher, Thomas Jefferson High School, Richmond, Virginia.

Zisowitz, Milton L., Head of the English Department, Haaren High School, New York.

2: *High Schools Visited*

Florida

Booker T. Washington High School, Miami
North Miami High School, Miami

Georgia

Oglethorpe High School, Oglethorpe

Illinois

Hyde Park High School, Chicago

Michigan

Central High School, Detroit

Cody High School, Detroit
Cooley High School, Detroit
Denby High School, Detroit
Miller High School, Detroit
Northeastern High School, Detroit
Northern High School, Detroit
Lincoln Junior High School, Warren
Lincoln Senior High School, Warren

New York

Haaren High School, New York
High School of Commerce, New York
Julia Richman High School, New York

Virginia

Armstrong High School, Richmond
Thomas Jefferson High School, Richmond

Washington, D. C.

Fairmont Heights High School, Prince George's County, Maryland

3: *Colleges and Universities Visited*

Atlanta University, Atlanta, Georgia
Bethune-Cookman College, Daytona Beach, Florida
Columbia University, New York
District of Columbia Teachers College, Washington, D. C.
Florida State University, Gainesville, Florida
Georgetown University, Institute of Language and Linguistics, Washington, D. C.
Michigan State University, East Lansing, Michigan
New York University, New York
Northwestern University, Evanston, Illinois
University of Chicago, Chicago
University of Miami, Miami, Florida
University of Michigan, Ann Arbor, Michigan
Wayne State University, Detroit

4: *Conventions and Conferences Attended*

Detroit English Club, April 21, 1955.

National Education Association Convention, Chicago, July 5-8, 1955.

Michigan Education Association Convention, Detroit, October 27, 28, 1955.

National Council of Teachers of English Convention, New York, November 24-26, 1955.

Michigan State Reading Conference, East Lansing, February 28, 29, 1956.

Democratic Human Relations Conference, Detroit, March 3, 1956.

Department of Audio-Visual Instruction National Convention, Detroit, March 12-16, 1956.

Eighth Annual Reading Conference, sponsored by the Department of Reading Efficiency and Study Skills, Wayne University, Detroit, March 24, 1956.

National Association of Foreign Student Advisers Convention, Washington, D. C., April 24, 1956.

The First Annual Meeting of the International Reading Association, Chicago, May 10-12, 1956.

University of Michigan Conference Series for English Teachers, Ann Arbor, June 25, July 2, 9, 16, 23, 30, 1956.

Bibliography

Adler, Catherine E. "Developing Oral Communication Skills," *English Journal*, XLI (1952), 24-30.

Allen, Harold B. "The Linguistic Atlases: Our New Resources," *English Journal*, XLV (1956), 188-94.

Anderson, Wallace L. "Structural Linguistics: Some Implications and Applications," *English Journal*, XLVI (1957), 410-18.

Ashmore, Harry S. *The Negro and the Schools.* Chapel Hill: University of North Carolina Press, 1954.

Atwood, Elmer Bagby. *A Survey of Verb Forms in the Eastern United States.* Ann Arbor: University of Michigan Press, 1953.

Babcock, C. Merton, Ed., *Syllabus Communication Skills.* East Lansing: Michigan State University Press, 1954.

Barrows, Marjorie Wescott. *Good English Through Practice.* New York: Henry Holt and Co., 1956.

Bender, James F., *How to Talk Well.* New York: McGraw-Hill Book Co., 1949.

Benson, W., and H. L. Helton. *Coding Techniques in Educational Research.* Detroit: Wayne State University, 1955. Mimeograph.

Bernard, Edward G., and Clifford Ettinger. *Using the Tape Recorder.* Curriculum Bulletin, 1952-53 Series, No. 6. New York: Board of Education of the City of New York, 1953.

Bettelheim, Bruno. *Overcoming Prejudice.* Chicago: Science Research Associates, 1953.

Billups, Edgar P. "Some Principles for the Representation of Negro Dialect in Fiction," *Texas Review*, VIII (1923), 99-123.

Birmingham, Anna I., and George Philip Krapp. *First Lessons in Speech Improvement.* New York: Charles Scribner's Sons, 1922.

Bond, Horace M. "Negro Education," in Walter S. Monroe, Ed., *Encyclopedia of Educational Research.* Rev. ed., New York: The Macmillan Co., 1950, pp. 777-95.

Boykin, Ulysses W. *A Handbook on the Detroit Negro.* Detroit: The Minority Study Associates, 1943.

Bram, Joseph. *Language and Society.* Garden City, New York: Doubleday & Co., 1955.

Britton, Jane. " Let Them Talk–The Community Will Listen! " *English Journal,* XLIV (1955), 159-60.

Brown, James I. " The Construction of a Diagnostic Test of Listening Comprehension," *Journal of Experimental Education,* XVIII (1949), 139-46.

Brueckner, Leo J. " Diagnosis in Teaching," in Walter S. Monroe, Ed., *Encyclopedia of Educational Research.* Rev. ed., New York: The Macmillan Co., 1950, pp. 314-21.

——— and Ernest O. Melby. *Diagnostic and Remedial Teaching.* New York: Houghton Mifflin Co., 1931.

Bullock, R. W. " A Study of Occupational Choice of Negro High School Boys," *Crisis,* XXXVII (1930), 301-03, 322.

Bunche, Ralph J. " Education in Black and White," *Journal of Negro Education,* V (1930), 351-58.

Burley, Dan. *Original Handbook of Harlem Jive.* New York: published by the author, 1944.

Christ, Henry I., Ed., *High Points in the Work of the High Schools of New York City.* New York: Board of Education of the City of New York, November, 1955.

Clapp, John M., Ed., *The Place of English in American Life.* Champaign, Ill.: National Council of Teachers of English, 1926.

Clary, Elizabeth, and Robert J. Dixon. *Pronunciation Exercises in English for the Foreign Born.* New York: Regents Publishing Co., 1947.

Cobbs, Hawner. " Negro Colloquialism in the Black Belt," *Alabama Review,* V (1952), 203-12.

Cook, Lloyd Allen. *Intergroup Relations in Teacher Education.* Washington: American Council on Education, 1951.

Courtis, Stuart A. " Growth and Development in Children," *Advances in Health Education,* Report of the Seventh Health Education Conference, Ann Arbor, 1934. New York: American Child Health Association, 1934, pp. 180-204.

———. " Of the Children, by the Children, for the Children," *Childhood Education,* XIV, No. 3 (1937), 101-05.

———. " The Status Index as a Measure of Individual Differences,"

The Twelfth Yearbook of the National Council on Measurements Used in Education, Part II (1955), 61-67.

Craigie, Sir William A., and James R. Hulbert. *A Dictionary of American English on Historical Principles.* 4 vols., Chicago: The University of Chicago Press, 1938-44.

Crobaugh, Clyde. "Haw, What a Hobby!" *Colliers,* CXXXVII, No. 5 (March 2, 1956), 48-49.

Crum, Mason. *Gullah; Negro Life in the Carolina Sea Islands.* Duke University Publications XV. Durham, N. Car.: Duke University Press, 1940.

Davis, Allison. *Children of Bondage: The Personality Development of Negro Youth in the Urban South.* Washington: American Council on Education, 1940.

———. *Social-Class Influences Upon Learning.* Cambridge: Harvard University Press, 1948.

———. "Socio-Economic Influence Upon Children's Learning," *School Life,* XXXIII (1951), 87, 93-94.

———, Burleigh B. Gardner, and Mary R. Gardner. *Deep South.* Chicago: University of Chicago Press, 1941.

——— and Robert D. Hess. "What About IQ's?" *National Education Association Journal,* XXXVIII (1949), 604-05.

Davis, Edith A. *The Development of Linguistic Skill in Twins, Singletons with Siblings, and Only Children from Age Five to Ten Years.* "Institute of Child Monographs Series," No. 14. Minneapolis: University of Minnesota Press, 1937.

Davis, Irene P. "The Speech Aspects of Reading Readiness," *Newer Practices in Reading in the Elementary School, Seventeenth Yearbook, Bulletin of the Department of Elementary School Principals, N. E. A.* Washington: National Education Association, 1938, pp. 282-89.

Dawson, Mildred A. "Interrelationships Between Speech and Other Language Arts Areas," in *Interrelationships Among the Language Arts.* Champaign, Ill.: The National Council of Teachers of English, 1954, pp. 23-33.

Day, Ella J. "The Development of Language in Twins: I. A Comparison of Twins and Single Children," *Child Development,* III (1932), 179-99.

DeBoer, John J., Walter V. Kaulfers, and Helen Rand Miller. *Teaching Secondary English.* New York: McGraw-Hill Book Co., 1951.

Dimmick, E. A. "Occupational Survey for Colored Boys in Pittsburgh," *School Education Journal,* V (1930), 138-47.

Dixon, C., and D. Shelley. "Let's Explore an Audio-Visual Approach to Correcting Speech and Hearing Difficulties," *National Education Association Journal,* XLIV (1955), 47-48.

Dixon, Robert J. *Exercises in English Conversation for the Foreign Born.* New York: Regents Publishing Co., 1945.

———. *Tests and Drills in English Grammar for Foreign Students.* New York: Latin-American Institute Press, 1949.

Dooley, Grace V., and Leontine A. Murtha. *Toward Better Speech.* New York: Board of Education of the City of New York, 1953.

Doran, Alicia T. "Retardation Among Negro Pupils in the Junior High School," *Journal of Negro Education,* V (1936), 228-31.

Dow, Clyde, Charles Irvin, and Ralph Renwick. *Improving Listening Comprehension.* East Lansing: Michigan State University Department of Communication Skills, n. d. Mimeograph.

Dunlap, Knight. *Personal Adjustment.* New York: McGraw-Hill Book Co., 1946.

Educational Policies Commission of the National Education Association. *Education for All American Youth.* Washington: National Education Association, 1944.

Education Service Department, Minnesota Mining and Manufacturing Co. *The Tape Recorder in the Elementary Classroom: A Handbook of Tested Uses.* St. Paul: Minnesota Mining and Mfg. Co., 1956.

Embree, Edwin. "Amazon of God," in Ruth M. Stauffer and William H. Cunningham, Eds., *Adventures in Modern Literature.* 3rd ed., New York: Harcourt, Brace and Co., 1953.

Ernst, Margaret S. *Words, English Roots and How They Grow.* New York: Alfred A. Knopf and Co., 1950.

Finder, Morris. "Teaching English to Slum-Dwelling Pupils," *English Journal,* XLIV (1955), 199-204, 242.

———. "Units Aplenty," *English Journal,* XLII (1953), 324-29.

Francis, W. Nelson. "Revolution in Grammar," *Quarterly Journal of Speech,* XL (1954), 299-312.

Fries, Charles C. *American English Grammar.* New York: Appleton-Century-Crofts, Inc., 1940.

———. *Patterns of English Sentences.* Ann Arbor; University of Michigan English Language Institute, 1953.

———. *The Structure of English.* New York: Harcourt, Brace and Co., 1952.

———. *The Teaching of the English Language.* New York: Thomas Nelson and Sons, 1927.

Gannon, Timothy J. *Psychology: The Unity of Human Behavior.* New York: Ginn and Co., 1954.

Gary, Nancy, Ed., *Department of English Course of Study and Points of Emphasis.* Richmond, Virginia: Thomas Jefferson High School, n. d. Mimeograph.

Gholson, G. James. Coordinator. *Resource Guide for Problems of Democratic Government.* Washington: Fairmont Heights High School, 1953. Mimeograph.

———. Coordinator. *Resource Guide for Problems of Intercultural Relations.* Washington: Fairmont Heights High School, 1953. Mimeograph.

———. Coordinator. *Resource Guide for Problems of Self-Understanding.* Washington: Fairmont Heights High School, 1953. Mimeograph.

———. Coordinator. *Resource Guide for Problems of Vocations and Employment.* Washington: Fairmont Heights High School, 1953. Mimeograph.

Gleason, H. A., Jr. *An Introduction to Descriptive Linguistics.* New York: Henry Holt and Co., 1955.

Gloster, Hugh M., William E. Farrison, and Nathaniel Tillman. *My Life, My Country, My World.* New York: Prentice-Hall, 1952.

Golden, Ruth I. *The 3 Book, Communication Skills.* Rev. ed., New Boston, Mich.: Huron Valley Lithographers, 1959.

Gray, Giles Wilkerson, and Claude Merton Wise. *The Bases of Speech.* New York: Harper and Brothers, 1934.

Greene, Harry A. "English–Language, Grammar and Composition," in Walter S. Monroe, Ed., *Encyclopedia of Educational Research.* Rev. ed., New York: The Macmillan Co., 1950, pp. 383-96.

Growing Pains in Grammar. The English Journal, XLVII, No. 4 (April, 1958).

Hale, L. L. "Your Speech Habits are Catching!" *National Education Association Journal,* XLIII (1954), 61-62.

Hall, Robert A., Jr. *Leave Your Language Alone!* Ithaca, New York: Linguistica, 1950.

Hardwick, H. C. *Words Are Important, First Book of Vocabulary Improvement.* New York: C. S. Hammond & Co., 1954.

Hatfield, Wilbur W. "Advances in the Teaching of English," *National Education Association Journal,* XLV (1956), 90-92.

Haugh, Oscar M. "The English Teacher as Teacher of Speech," *English Journal,* XLIV (1955), 205-10.

Hayakawa, S. I. *Language in Action.* New York: Harcourt, Brace and Co., 1941.

———. *Language in Thought and Action.* New York: Harcourt, Brace and Co., 1949.

Herman, Lewis Helmar, and Marguerite Shalett Herman. *Manual of American Dialects for Radio, Stage and Screen.* Chicago: Ziff Davis Publishing Co., 1947.

Hirsch, Ruth. *Audio-Visual Aids in Language Teaching.* Washington: Georgetown University Press, 1954.

Horwill, Herbert William. *A Dictionary of Modern American Usage.* London: Oxford University Press, 1935.

Huggard, Ethel F. *Suggestions to Teachers of Experimental Core Classes. Curriculum Bulletin,* 1950-51 Series, No. 2. New York: Board of Education of the City of New York, 1951.

Hughes, Langston. *The First Book of Negroes.* New York: Franklin Watts, 1952.

Human Relations in Secondary Education. The Bulletin of the National Association of Secondary-School Principals, XXXIX, No. 209 (1955).

Hyte, Charles. "Occupational Interests of Negro High School Boys," *School Review,* XLIV (1936), 34-40.

Jennings, Frank G. "Hidden Hungers: The Care and Feeding of the Young Reader." Address at the Book Manufacturers' Institute Convention at White Sulphur Springs, West Virginia, October 14, 1955.

Jesperson, Otto. *The Philosophy of Grammar.* New York: Henry Holt and Co., 1924.

Johnson, C. S. "'On the Need of Realism in Negro Education," *Journal of Negro Education,* V (1936), 375-82.

Kegler, Stanley B. "Techniques in Teaching Listening for Main Ideas," *English Journal,* XLV (1956), 30-32.

Keller, Fred S., and William N. Schoenfeld. *Principles of Psychology.* New York: Appleton-Century-Crofts, Inc., 1950.

Keller, James. *All God's Children.* New York: Christopher Books, 1953.

Kelly, F. J., Director. *National Survey of the Higher Education of Negroes. General Studies of Colleges for Negroes,* Misc. No. 6, Vol. II. Washington: Office of Education, 1942.

Kennedy, Arthur G. *English Usage.* New York: D. Appleton-Century Co., 1942.

Kenyon, John S. "Levels of Speech and Colloquial English," *English Journal,* XXXVII (1948), 25-31.

———. "*Weh-heh* Smiler!" *American Speech,* XXVI (1951), 309-10.

———. "*Will* of Inanimate Volition," *American Speech,* XXIII (1948), 10-28.

Ketchum, Roland and Jay E. Green. *Improving Your Vocabulary and Spelling.* New York: Noble and Noble, 1945.

Klapper, Paul. *Teaching English in Elementary and Junior High Schools.* New York: D. Appleton and Co., 1925.

Krapp, George Philip. "The English of the Negro," *The American Mercury,* II (1924), 190-95.

Kurath, Hans. *American Pronunciation.* Society for Pure English Tract No. XXX. London: Clarendon Press, 1928.

———, Ed., *Linguistic Atlas of New England.* Providence: Brown University, 1939-43.

LaBrant, Lou. *We Teach English.* New York: Harcourt, Brace and Co., 1951.

Laird, Charlton. *The Miracle of Language.* New York: Fawcett World Library (Premier Books), 1957.

Leonard, Sterling A. *Current English Usage,* English Monograph, No. 1. Champaign, Ill.: National Council of Teachers of English, 1932.

Lewis, Norman. *How to Read Better and Faster.* Rev. ed., New York: Thomas Y. Crowell Co., 1955.

———. *Word Power Made Easy.* Garden City, New York: Doubleday and Co., 1949.

Lloyd, Donald J. "The Implications of Linguistics for the Teaching of English," Address at the Middle Atlantic College English Association. Washington, May 2, 1953; in the *CEA Critic,* XVI, No. 3 (March, 1954), 4.

——— and Harry R. Warfel. *American English in Its Cultural Setting.* New York: Alfred A. Knopf and Co., 1956.

Lyman, R. L. *Summary of Investigations Relating to Grammar, Language, and Composition.* Supplementary Educational Monographs, No. 36. Chicago: University of Chicago Press, 1929.

Mallay, Helena. "A Study of Some of the Techniques Underlining the Establishment of Successful Social Contacts at the Preschool Level," *Journal of Genetic Psychology,* XLVII (1935), 431-57.

Mallis, Jackie. "An Experiment with the New Grammar," *English Journal,* XLVI (1957), 425-27.

Malmstrom, Jean. "A Study of the Validity of Textbook Statements about Certain Controversial Grammatical Items in the Light of Evidence from the Linguistic Atlas," Ph. D. dissertation, University of Minnesota, 1958.

Marckwardt, Albert H., and Fred Walcott. *Facts About Current English Usage.* English Monograph No. 7, National Council of Teachers of English. New York: Appleton-Century-Crofts, Inc., 1938.

Mathews, Mitford M., Ed., *A Dictionary of Americanisms On Historical Principles.* Chicago: The University of Chicago Press, 1951.

Mauk, Grant. "Speak Up!" *English Journal,* XLIV (1955), 290-91.

McCarthy, Dorothea. "Child Development: Language," in Walter S. Monroe, Ed., *Encyclopedia of Educational Research.* Rev. ed., New York: The Macmillan Co., 1950, pp. 165-72.

McCloskey, Mark A. *Manual for Teachers of Adult Elementary Classes.* New York: Board of Education of the City of New York, 1950.

McDavid, Raven I., Jr. "Two Decades of the Linguistic Atlas," *Journal of English and Germanic Philology,* L (1951), 101-10.

———. "Derivatives of Middle English [o:] in the South Atlantic Area," *Quarterly Journal of Speech,* XXXV (1949), 496-504.

——— and Virginia Glenn McDavid. "The Relationship of the Speech of American Negroes to the Speech of Whites," *American Speech,* XXVI (1951), 3-17.

Miller, Ward S. *Word Wealth.* New York: Henry Holt and Co., 1958.

Morgan, Lucia C. *Voice and Diction Drill Book for Students in Speech.* Dubuque, Iowa: William C. Brown Co., 1954.

Myrdal, Gunnar, Richard Sterner, and Arnold Rose. *An American Dilemma.* 2 vols., New York: Harper and Brothers, 1944.

National Conference on Research in English. *Interrelationships Among the Language Arts.* Champaign, Ill.: National Council of Teachers of English, 1954.

National Council of Teachers of English Commission on the English Curriculum. *The English Language Arts.* New York: Appleton-Century-Crofts, Inc., 1952.

National Council of Teachers of English Commission on the English Curriculum. *The English Language Arts in the Secondary School.* New York: Appleton-Century-Crofts, Inc., 1956.

Nixon, John E. *The Mechanics of Questionnaire Construction.* Detroit: Wayne University, 1952, Mimeograph, Reprinted from Walter S. Monroe, Ed., *Encyclopedia of Educational Research.* Rev. ed., New York: The Macmillan Co., 1950, pp. 948-51.

Olson, H. F. " Speech for All," *English Journal,* XL (1951), 204-09.

Onica, Paul G. " A Study of Certain Substandard English Usage Habits: Some Causes and Suggested Remedial Procedures." Master's thesis, Wayne University, 1954.

Ottley, Roi. " Mass Migration of Negroes from Rural Areas of the South to Industrial Centers in the North," *The Detroit Free Press.* A series of articles, May 27-June 8, 1956.

Partridge, Eric. *A Dictionary of Slang and Unconventional English.* New York: The Macmillan Co., 1950.

Peare, Catherine Owens. *Mary McLeod Bethune.* New York: The Vanguard Press, 1951.

Pettit, Maurice L. " Should We Give Up On High School English? " *Bulletin of the National Association of Secondary-School Principals,* XXXIX (1955), 133-37.

Pooley, Robert C. " Looking Ahead in Grammar," *Education Digest,* XXI (1955), 24-26.

———. *Teaching English Usage.* New York: Appleton-Century-Crofts, Inc., 1946.

Population, Housing and Economic Characteristics of the Detroit Standard Metropolitan Area—1957. Detroit: *The Detroit News,* 1958.

Prater, Clifford H., Jr. *Manual of American English Pronunciation for Adult Foreign Students.* Los Angeles: University of California Press, 1951.

Prince, John Dyneley. " Surinam Negro-English," *American Speech*, IX, (1934), 181-86.

Roberts, Paul. *Patterns of English*. New York: Harcourt, Brace and Co., 1956.

———. *Understanding English*. New York: Harper and Brothers, 1958.

Rollins, Charlemae. *We Build Together*. Rev. ed. Champaign, Ill.: National Council of Teachers of English, 1948.

Rossiter, A. P. *Our Living Language*. London: Longmans, Green and Co., 1952.

Russell, David H. " We all Need to Read," *Saturday Review*, XXXIX, No. 7 (February 18, 1956), 36.

Schenberg, Samuel, Coordinator. *Handbook of Procedures for Teachers of Adults in the Evening High Schools of New York City*. Curriculum Bulletin, 1953-54 Series, No. 9. New York: Board of Education of the City of New York, 1954.

Schmidt, Bernadine G. " Language Development as an Aid to the Social Adjustment of Mental Defectives," *Mental Hygiene*, XXV (1941), 402-13.

Schofield, Ruth E. " Some Thoughts on Oral Language," *Education Digest*, XXI (1955), 50-52.

Senatore, John J. " SVO: A Key to Clearer Language Teaching," *English Journal*, XLVI (1957), 419-24.

Shaftel, George and Fannie R. Shaftel. *Role Playing the Problem Story*. New York: National Conference of Christians and Jews, 1952.

Shane, Harold G. *Research Helps in Teaching the Language Arts*. Washington: Association for Supervision and Curriculum Development, 1955.

Smith, A. M. " Negro Life in Detroit," *The Detroit News*. January 28-February 12, 1946.

Smith, Dora V. " English Grammar Again! " *English Journal*, XXVII (1938), 643-48.

Smith, Logan Pearsall. *The English Language*. 2nd ed., London: Oxford University Press, 1952.

Speech Association of America. *Check List of Books and Equipment in Speech from the 1956 Annual Directory*. Baton Rouge: Louisiana State University Press, 1956.

Sutherland, Robert Lee. *Color, Class and Personality*. Washington: American Council on Education, 1942.

Symonds, Percival M. "Practice *versus* Grammar in the Learning or Correct English Usage," *Journal of Educational Psychology,* XXII (1931), 81-95.

Tape Recording Magazine. I (April, 1956).

Taylor, Florence. *Why Stay in School?* Chicago: Science Research Associates, 1949.

Taylor, Grant. *Learning American English.* New York: Saxon Press, 1954.

The 5th Quinquennial Survey of the Detroit Market. Detroit: *The Detroit News,* 1957, p. 10.

The Teaching of Language. The English Journal, XLV, No. 4 (April, 1956).

Trager, George L., and Henry Lee Smith, Jr. *An Outline of English Structure.* Washington: American Council of Learned Societies, 1957.

Trow, William Clark. *The Learning Process:* "What Research Says to the Teacher," No. 6. Washington: Department of Classroom Teachers, American Educational Research Association of the National Educational Association, 1954.

Turner, Lorenzo D. "Problems Confronting the Investigator of Gullah," *American Dialect Society Publications,* IX (1947), 74-84.

United Community Services of Metropolitan Detroit Research Department. *Social Rating of Community Areas in Detroit.* Detroit: United Community Services, 1955.

Van Patten, Nathan. "The Vocabulary of the American Negro as Set Forth in Contemporary Literature," *American Speech,* VII (1931), 24-31.

Van Riper, C. *You Can Talk Better.* Chicago: Science Research Associates, 1953.

Waldhorn, Arthur, and Arther Zeiger. *English Made Simple.* New York: Made Simple Books, 1955.

Walsh, J. Martyn, and Anna Kathleen Walsh. *Plain English Handbook.* Wichita, Kansas: McCormick Mathers, 1939.

Watkins, Rhoda, and Eda B. Frost. *Your Speech and Mine.* Chicago: Lyons and Carnahan, 1956.

White, Morris. *Concise Survey of High School English.* New York: Oxford Book Co., 1955.

Whorf, Benjamin Lee. *Collected Papers on Metalinguistics.* Washington: Department of State, Foreign Service Institute, 1952.

Wilkerson, D. A. "The Peculiar Problems of Negroes in American Social Life," *Journal of Negro Education,* V (1930), 324-50.

Wilson, George P., Ed., *Word-Lists From the South.* Publications American Dialect Society, No. 2. Greensboro, N. Car., 1944.

Wolfarth, Julia H. *Self-Help Methods of Teaching English.* New York: Yonkers-on-Hudson Co., 1905.

Woodson, Carter Godwin. *The Story of the Negro Retold.* 3rd. ed., Washington: The Associated Publishers, 1945.

Woofter, Thomas Jackson, Jr. *Races and Ethnic Groups in American Life.* New York: McGraw-Hill Book Co., 1933.

Wright, Audrey L. *Practice Your English.* New York: American Book Co., 1952.

Young, Florence M. "An Analysis of Certain Variables in a Developmental Study of Language," *Genetic Psychology,* XXIII (1941), 3-141.

Index of Topics

Index of Names

Edited by Alexander Brede
Designed by Sylvia Winter
Set in Baskerville and Bulmer type faces
Printed on Warren's Olde Style Antique Wove paper
Bound in Strathmore Beau Brilliant Newport Blue
Manufactured in the United States of America